Charisma

The secrets of making a lasting impression

Andrew Leigh

Prentice Hall Life
is an imprint of

Harlow, England • London • New York • Boston • San Francisco • Toronto
Sydney • Tokyo • Singapore • Hong Kong • Seoul • Taipei • New Delhi
Cape Town • Madrid • Mexico City • Amsterdam • Munich • Paris • Milan

PEARSON EDUCATION LIMITED

Edinburgh Gate
Harlow CM20 2JE
Tel: +44 (0)1279 623623
Fax: +44 (0)1279 431059
Website: www.pearson.com/uk

First published in Great Britain in 2008 as *The Charisma Effect*
Second edition published as *Charisma* 2011

ISBN: 978-0-273-76158-7

British Library Cataloguing-in-Publication Data
A catalogue record for this book is available from the British Library

Library of Congress Cataloging-in-Publication Data
A catalog record for this book is available from the Library of Congress

10 9 8 7 6 5 4 3 2
15 14 13 12 11

Typeset in 10/14 Plantin by 30
Printed in Great Britain by Henry Ling Limited, at the Dorset Press, Dorchester, DT1 1HD

Contents

About the author

Andrew Leigh is a founding director of Maynard Leigh Associates, the development and consultancy service whose mission is to unlock people's potential.

For some years he was a business feature writer on *The Observer* and later worked for many years as an Assistant Director in the public sector. Author of more than a dozen books on management, leadership and presentation, he is a Fellow of the Chartered Institute of Personnel and Development.

Acknowledgements

Charisma reflects contributions from various people who have kindly read drafts, commented or assisted in some way. In particular, I am grateful to:

- Henry Stewart of Happy Ltd who helped set the whole idea in motion;
- the following from Maynard Leigh Associates: my fellow Director Michael Maynard, for his usual full and thoughtful observations; Bridget Brice, Director of the Personal Impact Course; Adrian Jones, Ann Walsh, Barbara Thorn, Bill Britten, Caroline Kennedy, Deena Gornick, John Spencer, Josie Maskell, Rosanna Mason, Steve Bolton and Siobhan Stamp;
- and from outside Maynard Leigh: Roger Taylor of T-Mobile, Ian Cutler of Skandia, Susan Coulson of Barclaycard, Simon Adams and Aiden Leigh.

Thanks also to Darion and Aiden Leigh for their technical help with the charisma-effect.com website.

Samantha Jackson of Pearson Education nursed this book from inception to its final publication and was always a support throughout.

Finally, I offer special thanks to Gillian Leigh who, despite her busy schedule, went far beyond the call of duty by providing many insightful improvements and suggestions.

Charisma is dedicated to Gilly.

Publisher's acknowledgements

We are grateful to the following for permission to reproduce copyright material:

Table

Table on page 10 from *Releasing your Hidden Charisma*, www.audiencewithcharisma.com (Owen, Nikki 2008) with permission.

Text

Quote on page 185–6 from Smile, though your party's breaking, *The Guardian*, 28 November 2007 (Hoggart, Simon), Copyright Guardian News & Media Ltd 2007

In some instances we have been unable to trace the owners of copyright material and we would appreciate any information that would enable us to do so.

Introduction

'The minute you walked in the joint, I could see you were a man of distinction. A real big spender.' This familiar lyric is a musical reminder that people tend to judge us in an eye blink. Therefore, it is hardly surprising that when it comes to making a memorable impression there is a popular belief that 'you've either got it or you haven't'.

This idea partly stems from larger than life characters that make an exceptional impression. These are the people commonly labelled 'charismatic'. They include film stars, politicians, generals, entrepreneurs, inventors and artists.

The idea that just about anyone can have charisma and make a memorable, lasting impression is therefore a tough one to sell. Just how memorable do you want to be, how lasting an impression do you want to achieve? And, what price would you pay to make an indelible impact on those you encounter? Not in terms of money, though that can buy useful professional help to strengthen your impact. I mean, how far are you willing to go in developing your natural, in-built charisma? If you are simply hungry for tips and techniques then, fine, there are plenty of those around already. However, if you could transform your charisma simply by collecting instant tips you would probably have done so by now.

how far are you willing to go in developing your natural, in-built charisma?

As one charisma expert puts it: 'You can't teach people charismatic skills without seeking to create a mindset change.'[1]

Instead of a collection of instant tips – seven ways to be more charismatic – we are going to be unravelling the DNA of charisma. This implies understanding what it really takes to strengthen it, so that you can enhance your presence, and gravitas. That is, you will start using your charisma's full potential to make a more memorable and lasting impression.

Did you ever see that great musical *Chicago*? The husband of the central character sings a terrific number in which he calls himself 'Mr Cellophane'. He complains people look right through him and hardly know he is there. On leaving the room about the only thing people notice about him is the door closing.

Mr Cellophane is at one end of the Charisma Spectrum. It is a charisma-free zone and, almost certainly, you are not at it. Only a tiny minority of people are truly Cellophane people, devoid of any personality and so charisma-challenged that they can never make an impact.

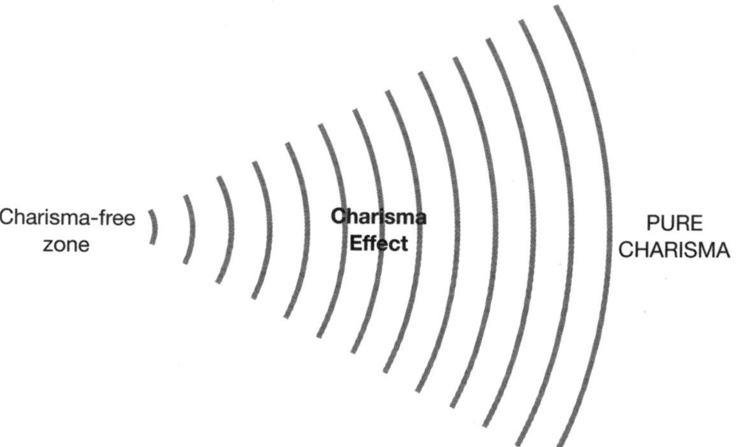

People right at the other end of the charisma spectrum literally transform people's lives. This is Extreme Charisma and if you possess it, you may move millions with your presence. Again, few of us fall into the category, or aspire to such heights.

Yes, it would be great to make the impact of say Obama or Elvis Presley, and there is certainly much to learn from them. Yet their Extreme Charisma is so rare and impactful that it distorts the whole meaning of charisma, moving it well beyond the reach of most of us.

Yet charisma in its rather less extreme form, called for clarification The Charisma Effect, is certainly learnable. You can steadily develop yours and make a strong, lasting impression on those you encounter.

As you become more familiar with what creates charisma, a number of questions may occur to you. For example, can you learn charisma or must you be born with it? What does charisma actually mean? What are the essential ingredients that create it? Do you need charisma to be an effective leader? We tackle these questions and others throughout the rest of this book.

You will encounter the essential ingredients that can enhance your Charisma Effect, though not produce Extreme Charisma, which we explore in the next chapter.

The early part of this book explores your charisma aims. These will affect how you come across to people and the impression you make.

Although in 1947 the renowned sociologist Max Weber saw charisma as a trait, more recent studies suggest it is a set of learnable behaviours. Many are about being yourself in how people experience you. We look at these in Part 2.

Part 3 dissects the more complex and opaque aspect of charisma usually called personal chemistry. You have only a limited control over personal chemistry but, as this section shows, you can certainly influence it.

Digging deeper in Part 4, we explore aspects of creating charisma that cross the boundary between being yourself and what creates personal chemistry. These include smiling, eye contact and body language, and what charisma means for leadership.

You may decide to read the book from start to finish and that is fine. Equally, you may prefer to focus on an area in which you already know you need to develop. Apart from a readiness to experiment with new ways of behaving, what matters most is your willingness to accept that you can indeed develop your charisma.

While you may be happy to improve your Charisma Effect, some of those around you might prefer you to stay the same. It is a bit like losing weight. You may want to do it, but others might actually prefer you fat and comfortable. So when it comes to actually changing, be prepared to meet resistance, if not in yourself maybe from others.

Part 1

Aim

Discover and clarify your real purpose

Chapter 1

Unravelling the DNA of charisma

Marilyn Monroe once went shopping with a friend who was amazed that no one seemed to recognise the star. Monroe explained it was because at that moment she was off-stage. To demonstrate, Monroe 'switched on' her star quality. Within a few minutes, people began mobbing her, demanding her autograph, jostling for a closer look.

What exactly did Monroe do that changed the situation so comprehensively – and so quickly? Almost certainly, among other actions, she began paying close attention to everyone around her, 'relating' to them so intensely that they became fully aware of her presence. As they responded, so did she. Soon her Extreme Charisma spread like ripples in a pool where a stone had been thrown into it. Previously she had quietly confined it to just her and her companion.

When are we 'on stage' and when are we 'off-stage'? As the above suggests, the answer depends on both the situation and what we choose to do with it. Apply for a job, for example, and you may believe that you are 'off-stage' because the interview has not yet begun. Yet the curtain goes up even before you press the buzzer, or walk through reception. People start judging you while you talk to the receptionist, when you shake hands or perhaps even while you are reading quietly, waiting for the interview to start.

Making a lasting impression, to produce a Charisma Effect on other people is about tapping into your natural ability to connect

> your personal impact *is* your charisma

with people and build a relationship with them. Your personal impact *is* your charisma and the two terms appear interchangeably throughout this book.

In claiming to show you ways to strengthen your charisma, I am not entirely alone. Others also report success at developing this capability, of enhancing how one comes across in a memorable way. For example, one approach claims that it happens mainly by using energy and through being fully alert to your surroundings, namely being present. Others rely on methods that are more basic. These include learning to make proper eye contact, encouraging smiling, or developing the ability to 'talk to anyone'. These are certainly important ingredients.

Upping your Charisma Effect, the impact you have on others, is both easier, yet more involved than just learning a technique. To make a more lasting impression than you do at present will demand more from you than a quick fix. It takes time and effort to experiment, uncover and exploit your natural charisma, yet you can certainly do it. You can improve your charisma if you invest in the approach outlined here. To sum up, it is a journey not a destination.

In the regular workshops run by Maynard Leigh for over 21 years, we have worked with many hundreds of people to show them how to make a stronger personal impact, to develop their charisma. This book sums up much of that experience for you to use, without attending a special learning event. However, if you get the chance to spend a day or more with an expert on the topic, you may be able to shorten the journey you take towards a stronger charisma.

First impressions

Ex-Chairman of Royal Mail Alan Leighton recalls an experience in one company where he traced the progress of 50 people over a ten-year period. Relatively young, they had progressed from junior positions to just below board level.

'The nearest thing we found to a common denominator,' says Leighton, 'was the first impression of the senior manager in the room when they recruited them – the gut feel. And that became part of the criteria that we recruited on – the first impression.'

The importance of first impressions is what drives so much effort in improving charisma. While in theory you never get a second chance to make a first impression, the reality is that you always have an opportunity to make the most of your charisma; you just have to take it.

Charisma defined

As usual, the Greeks had a word for it. Charisma originated with an ancient Greek word meaning 'gift'.

The early Christians later used it to describe 'gifts from God that allowed receivers to carry out extraordinary feats such as healing and prophesy.'

So, in the more traditional sense, Extreme Charisma usually means an unusual ability to influence people and arouse devotion.

Today charisma usually means:

The ability to use all aspects of yourself to achieve a strong, memorable impact on other people, influencing them emotionally, physically, and intellectually, including their thoughts, attitudes and behaviour.

If you want an even handier handle, charisma is using your personality to make a powerful and memorable impression on people.

Signs your charisma needs attention

- I don't feel people really listen to me in meetings.
- I get offered jobs or projects below my level of ability and training.
- I hate giving a presentation or a talk.
- I feel uncomfortable looking people straight in the eye when I talk to them.
- People often ask me to repeat what I have said.
- People fidget, interrupt or look away when I speak.
- I have trouble getting my ideas accepted at work.
- In informal business situations requiring small talk, I feel tongue-tied and awkward.
- People often tell me I have picked the wrong time or place to bring up a certain subject.
- Whenever people offer advice or suggestions on my impact, usually I say 'yes, but...'.
- I often feel on the defensive with people.
- I find it hard to get others to co-operate with me.
- I don't really care about having a high profile, it's substance that counts.
- I have trouble remembering people's names, even after I've just been introduced.
- I'm not a joiner, I'd rather be alone.
- In meetings I like to sit where I won't be much noticed.
- When I enter a room I tend to hesitate, walk slowly and keep my head down.
- My facial expressions do not usually match my feelings.
- I tend to be late for appointments, I'm not a good time keeper.
- I find it really hard to make decisions, I have lots of self-doubt.

If any of these describe you, it's time to polish your charisma.

Extreme Charisma

For a while, during the early part of the twentieth century, the most famous woman in the world was the blind and deaf Helen Keller, who even had problems speaking clearly. Many entering her presence broke down in tears at the encounter, yet Helen herself did little to precipitate this reaction, except bear herself with great poise and dignity.

As mentioned earlier, Extreme Charisma lies at the far end of the Charisma Spectrum and is closer to the original meaning of charisma being something magical or a 'gift from God'.

Few of us encounter Extreme Charisma at first hand. Those with Extreme Charisma transform people's lives. Depending on your age, those at the far end of the Charisma Spectrum might include Jesus, Nelson Mandela, Madonna, Michael Jackson, Winston Churchill, Steve Jobs, Oprah Winfrey, and so on.

The extreme charismatic does what those who merely have a strong Charisma Effect do, only more so. Analysing four 'giants' with extreme charisma – Martin Luther King, Margaret Thatcher, Elvis Presley and Muhammad Ali – charisma expert Nikki Owen found they had only a few external characteristics in common between them. (See next page.)

There have been many attempts to demystify Extreme Charisma, mainly by listing some of the obvious and perhaps less obvious techniques. However, it defies an entirely objective or rational explanation as to exactly how extreme charismatics make such a profound impact. A simple list of what they do is never enough. It is rather like a scientist offering a detailed description of the mechanics of what it means to fall in love; there may be plenty of tangible evidence such as pupil dilation, increased heart rate, fast, shallow breathing and so on, but knowing it does not then enable you to fall in love.

External factors	King	Thatcher	Elvis	Ali
Eye contact	★★		★★★	★★★
Animated facial expression	★	★★	★★★	★★★
Uses strong hand gestures	★	★★	★★★	★★★
Natural smile				
Varied voice tone and pace	★★★	★	★★	★★
Fast talking pace	★		★	★★★
Commanding voice tonality	★★		★★★	★★
Use of pauses	★★	★	★	★★★
Centred body posture	★★★	★★	★★★	★★★
Clear diction	★★★	★	★★★	★
Actively listens	★★	★	★★	★
Large vocabulary	★★★	★	★★★	★★
Adaptable	★★	★	★★	★★
High physical energy	★★★	★★★	★★★	★★★
Appears enthusiastic	★★★	★★★	★★★	★★★
Open body language	★★	★	★★★	★★★
Resonant voice	★★★	★★	★★★	★★
Appears confident	★★★	★★★	★★★	★★★
Expert on their subject	★★★	★★★	★★★	★★★
Uses stories and metaphors	★★★	★	★★	★★★
Shows conviction	★★★	★★★	★★★	★★★

Reproduced with permission from *Releasing Your Hidden Charisma*, by Nikki Owen (2008), wwwaudiencewithcharisma.com

The cult of celebrity and massive media coverage further muddy the waters. It is often unclear how far fame and notoriety create charisma or vice versa. 'I can't untie the threads of how much I played up to the part that was written for me', is how Rolling Stones' guitarist Keith Richards puts it. 'I think in a way your persona, your image, as it used to be known, is like a ball and chain... people loved that image. They imagined me, they made me, the folks out there created this folk hero.'

Others such as The Beatles, Michael Jackson and Ghandi may reach millions around the world, yet may not prove to be particularly charismatic when you actually meet them. Close up, many of those blessed, or perhaps cursed, with Extreme Charisma turn out to be less impactful than you might expect, or have feet of clay.

You can even possess many of the attributes of an extreme charismatic without necessarily being particularly charismatic. For example, Richard Nixon was a powerful speaker with a compelling voice who rose from the ashes of ignominious defeat to become President. Yet close up the man was hardly charismatic, mainly achieving his political results through relentless hard work.

A colleague of ours tells how on a flight to India a grumpy man with an excessively brightly lit iPad annoyed other passengers trying to sleep. This man was also constantly rude and demanding of the cabin crew. Later he turned out to be a globally renowned CEO, particularly known for his caring approach to staff.

Paul Newman was married to actor Joanne Woodward for 50 years until his death. She complained that she did not see what everyone else saw in Paul Newman. He was entirely normal in his everyday life and his charisma was low-key. In fact, for many years while he was a successful racing driver, fellow racers did not even realise that he was *the* Paul Newman. Yet, when he was honoured with an award or appeared as himself in front of crowds, Newman visibly transformed.

Persuasion

While you may not aspire to demonstrating Extreme Charisma, some of the ingredients that create it are certainly available to you. They include knowing what you want to achieve, giving unusual eye contact, authenticity, attractive body language, vitality, smiling, exceptional empathy, and so on. One of the most critical ingredients is the ability to persuade – through words, voice and personal presence.

Even with the most exotic charismatics, their power of mass persuasion seldom occurs at the flick of a switch. Instead, it usually requires repeated exposure to the person.

The popular image of the great persuader is someone with an overwhelming personality who talks tough, strongly states their position, almost hits people over the head with their arguments, and ruthlessly pushes their point of view. This treats persuasion like a boxing match, won by the fiercest competitor.

In fact, persuasion is different. It is more like teaching than boxing. Extreme charismatic persuaders move people step-by-step to a solution, helping them appreciate why the position they advocate solves the problem best.

They incorporate into their persuasion not merely colourful and attractive language, including stories and metaphors, they also know the importance of using symbols with rich, cultural meanings. These include words like freedom, justice and equality; non-verbal signs might be the flag, Star of David, or Holy Cross; and images that are instantly recognised and processed like the Nike Swoosh or McDonald's Golden Arches. Symbols are persuaders' tools, harnessed to change attitudes and real meanings.

This combination of methods of persuasion partly explains why those with Extreme Charisma often regard themselves as teachers, rather than seeing themselves as more prosaic politicians, religious leaders, or directors.

Good charisma, bad charisma

> if you possess Extreme Charisma can you do more harm than good in the world?

Start delving into charisma and fairly soon you bump into the dilemma of whether the extreme version involves integrity or has an ethical dimension. More simply, if you possess Extreme Charisma can you do more harm than good in the world?

History is stuffed full of charismatic killers whose personality made a huge impact on many people, yet damaged lives rather than transformed them in a positive way. They include psychopaths who, rather than relying on their strength of personality for making an impact, instead used coercion and highly unethical behaviour to get their way. Past maniacs with Extreme Charisma who did more damage than good include Genghis Khan, Caligula, Al Capone, Hitler, Stalin, Mao, Saddam Hussein, and Pol Pot.

Charismatic megalomaniacs also usually take the helm of killer cults, like Charles Manson and The Family. Drunk with lust and power, they exercise physical and sexual control over their followers. In most cases, the beliefs of these deranged leaders stem from twisted interpretations of established doctrines.

The ethical dimension – can you be an extreme charismatic and do harm? – bedevils the whole field of charisma, leading to interesting but ultimately futile arguments about whether a particularly notorious character showed genuine Extreme Charisma or merely a distorted version of it.

Ultimately, charisma alone is not enough; you also need to show both character and competence. The former means you choose ethical uses for your charisma, not unethical ones. For example:

Ethical	Non-ethical
• Serve others	• Use others
• Use for mutual benefit	• Use for selfish interests
• Empower people	• Force people
• Open up communications	• Close down communication
• Follow the heart	• Follow the money, power or greed
• Interested in self	• Interested in others

Ultimately, we each have to arrive at a personal judgement about good and 'bad' charisma. This book assumes that charisma is neither good nor bad in itself; what matters is how you use it.

DNA of charisma

At our regular Personal Impact workshops, when we ask people 'What do you mean by impact?' they sometimes reply, 'It's all about clothes, smiling, eye contact and grooming'. Nor are they entirely wrong. These elements do affect how you come across – sometimes in a major way. The judgement people make of us occurs so quickly it's no wonder image consultants tout expensive advice on appearance and what colours to wear. Yet these are only the more obvious aspects of what creates charisma.

One of the less obvious is your ability to relate to people. Even the most fanatical techie, engrossed computer geek, or dedicated specialist to some extent cannot avoid dealing with people. For most of us, interacting with other people is a normal part of our daily lives, whether at home, at meetings, seeing the boss in the corridor, talking to a client, having a job interview, making a phone call, or being in a team.

In our digital age of texting, video conferencing and social networking, it can seem that actual interactions face-to-face with live human beings is on the decline. But all these trends merely put an even bigger premium on the quality of our relationships, and make the times we do interact with people even more critical.

When you come across well, people listen to you, notice what you say, seek your views, respond to your requests and so on. When your charisma is strong you are not merely present, you also have presence. Making this kind of impact involves three inseparables: the A-B-C of charisma.

- Aim – what you want to achieve.
- Be Yourself – specific behaviour traits.
- Chemistry – interactions and relationships.

They are inseparable because each affects the other and in doing so influences the person trying to make an impact. Here is a visual way of putting it:

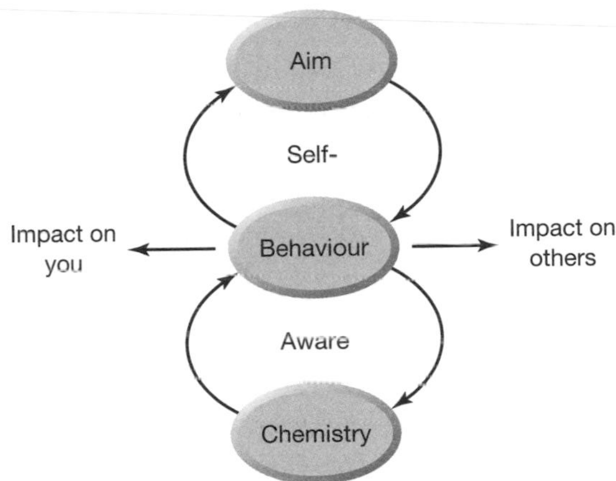

Your charisma aim affects your behaviour and ultimately how others behave. Behaviour, both yours and that of others, affects the chemistry between two people. In other words, there is a continuous feedback loop that occurs when someone is using their charisma.

For example, gestures such as nodding and other signs of listening stimulate this feedback loop and help people to bond. 'It's like being engaged in a synchronous dance', is how one charisma expert puts it.

While you have considerable control over your charisma aims, and how you behave, you can only expect to influence other people's behaviour and the resulting chemistry between you. The whole interactive process involves awareness of both self and others.

To improve your charisma therefore means learning more about these three interlinked elements of aim, behaviour and chemistry and how you can modify them.

We will be constantly referring to this route to improving charisma, so here is a shorthand way to sum it up. This makes it easier to remember during your day-to-day interactions with people.

When was the last time you were at your best and made a strong impression? Try completing the Charisma work out below and see whether this reveals anything interesting about your current Charisma Effect on others.

Charisma work out

1 Choose someone who impresses you with an ability to convey charisma; that is, to achieve a noticeable, strong personal impact.

   Preferably, choose someone you know, rather than some distant celebrity figure such as a TV personality, sportsperson or movie star.

2 List all the things about them that you feel produces their Charisma Effect.

Name of person:
What is it about them that contributes to their Charisma Effect? Why do they seem to make a positive and lasting impression? For example: They are direct; challenging; charming; etc. Be as specific as you can.
•
•
•
•
•
•
•
•

3 How many of these things about this person concern their actual behaviour and how many can be explained by intangibles such as personal chemistry?

Did you have trouble identifying when you made a strong impression? Think about a time when you got a job, had a romance, met people on holiday, completed a project and so on.

Experiment

Charisma is partly innate and partly a matter of applied learning. Virtually everyone can unlock their charisma potential and the main requirement, apart from adopting a more systematic approach, is deceptively simple: be willing to experiment.

> charisma is partly innate and partly a matter of applied learning

Experimenting does not mean you need to become an entirely different person, or alter your basic personality – you will still be you, though you may feel a new sense of confidence after trying new ways of behaving. It is in fact about your willingness to try new ideas, to explore new behaviours, to find ways to raise your self-awareness about the impact you actually make. Jacqueline Gold, persuasive head of the Ann Summers chain of shops, sums it up succinctly: 'Challenge yourself and great things will happen.'

You may be tempted to assume you will start applying some of the ideas and suggestions in this book only once you have read it all. That is rather like one of our participants on our Personal Impact course who, when asked some weeks afterwards, how it was going replied: 'Well, fine, but I haven't had a chance to use it yet.'

Developing your charisma requires you to keep working at it. Find daily ways to practise and experiment. Even small changes in how you behave can have surprisingly encouraging consequences. Look for opportunities to try out some of the ideas presented here whenever you have contact with other people, on the phone, in a store, with friends at a restaurant, travelling, in meetings, around the drinks machine – anywhere.

The self-awareness that underpins charisma requires you to stay alert and take notice of what is happening in the moment, especially when experimenting. A commentator who successfully tried out mirroring (see Chapter 12), for example, also complained bitterly about the 'state of mental confusion into which I am plunged whenever I try to hold a conversation and, at the same time, monitor and modify my own contribution to it.'

The solution is plenty of practice and experimentation. There is nothing instant about your charisma makeover; it inevitably takes time. People with charisma manage time well, whether in deciding how much of it to devote to each interaction, or the amount of effort they put into preparing for each encounter.

> *'It's never too late to be what you might have been.'*
>
> George Eliot, writer

Chapter 2

Charisma

Aim

'Mad dogs and Englishmen go out in the midday sun', carolled composer, singer, playwright, performer, author and inveterate traveller Noël Coward in his trademark, widely recognised, over-the-top manner.

Coward's forceful, showy and curious charisma bowled over many people he encountered; some misguided ones even tried to emulate him, usually with dismal results. Yet his memoirs reveal exhausted soldiers and unresponsive fellow passengers all found his unusual charisma unattractive. When he tried to be humorous, Coward found to his dismay that sometimes those on the receiving end failed to understand what he was trying to communicate.

As with Noël Coward, every communication situation involves both:

- Aim and audience.

These are merely two sides of the same coin when it comes to improving your Charisma Effect. Knowing what you want to achieve, and with whom, will be an important starting point in strengthening it.

Driven by vision

'Vision without execution is hallucination.'

Thomas A. Edison

If people with a strong charisma possess anything else in common, it is surely what President Bush Snr ruefully called the 'vision thing', knowing he sorely lacked it, along with charisma.

Vision drives charismatics. In some form, they hold a vivid picture in their minds of what they want to achieve.

For Thomas Watson, the joint discoverer of DNA, his vision at over 80 years old is a cure for cancer. For Alexander the Great, it was conquering the entire world. Florence Nightingale lived and breathed her aim of preventing unnecessary deaths after battle; Joan of Arc spoke movingly of her vision of France free of English rule and died for it.

Oscar Wilde had a hunger for maximum self-advertisement, while not actually doing that much, but it powered his undoubted charisma. Wilde claimed he had not walked the streets of London carrying a lily but had merely made the world believe that he did – a far more difficult feat.

'I have a dream' is how Martin Luther King famously spoke of his vision, while President Kennedy articulated his as a national challenge of epic proportions: the powerful image of 'putting a man on the moon by the end of the decade.'

Vision is the fuel of charisma. The bigger your vision the more it fires your charisma to communicate, excite, and enrol others in it.

> vision is a rather grand word for 'knowing what you want to achieve'

In reality, vision is a rather grand word for 'knowing what you want to achieve.' Revealingly, George Bush's contemptuous response about vision came when a friend suggested it would be sensible to go away to Camp David to decide where he wanted to take the country.

To strengthen your charisma, refine the stuff that fuels it: your aim. En route to clarifying what you want to achieve with your charisma, you may find it helpful to:

- Decide how you would like to be seen by others, and
- Discover how you actually are seen by others.

How you want to be seen by others

In our daily lives many of us choose to don a mask. We do not allow others to see the real person behind it; the mask conceals what we feel, hiding our fear of what people might actually see, such as our sense of inadequacy, or our uncertain communication aim.

On this journey to strengthening your charisma, you may need to explore what your particular mask looks like, and what lies behind it. Try the Behind the mask work out, shown below.

Behind the mask work out

1. First, consider how you would *like* to be seen by others.
2. In the left-hand column overleaf, write five to eight descriptions. For example:

   Happy, tough, punctual, thorough, dedicated, funny, honest, organised, clever, thoughtful, cheeky, bubbly.
3. Give careful thought to the ones you choose.
4. Next, consider how you *fear* you come across to others. For example, might they see you as:

   Ruthless, ambitious, funny, careless, rude, clumsy, late, immature?

5 Review the two lists together. What do they reveal about your likes and fears? How accurate do you think they are? Which is least desirable and which is the most?

6 Are there any surprises?

How I'd like to be seen	How I fear I'm seen
....	....
....	....
....	....
....	....
....	....
....	....
....	....
....	....

7 How accurate do you think the two lists you made really are?

Because they experience you in real life, other people can provide you with an important reality check. For example, you may feel you come across as quiet and thoughtful, yet those you encounter may describe you as aloof. Alternatively, you may believe you are funny and superficial, while those who meet you in real life might experience you as serious and thoughtful.

Your Charisma Rating

As part of refining your Charisma Aim, check out your Charisma Rating – how others actually *do* see you.

Rather than speculate on the impact of your charisma, systematically gather facts and evidence about how others experience you. Seeking out this kind of information may feel uncomfortable, yet it is one way to start putting your Charisma Aim on a sounder footing.

An alternative might be to attend a specialist workshop on charisma, when you will also receive a reality check on your developmental needs.

The Fast Reality Check Out described here uses seven basic behaviours which are common to those with strong personal impact. There are, of course, others and we will explore some of these throughout the rest of this book.

To discover your charisma rating, you need to approach people you trust to learn how they experience you. People love to help and if you can overcome your natural reluctance to ask for it, then you will gain immeasurably from the resulting feedback.

There is nothing shameful about wanting to strengthen your charisma. You may not want to call it that when you approach people for feedback; you might choose instead to talk of 'wanting to improve my personal impact with people.'

First, complete the questionnaire below for yourself. Later you can compare your charisma rating with how others experience you.

Secondly, choose up to five people you know and trust to give you frank answers. Give or send them the questionnaire below. This whole process can also be done online, including obtaining an analysis of the results – contact Maynard Leigh Associates.

Fast reality check out

I am exploring the personal impact I make on people – that is, how I come across.

Please be as frank as possible, scoring me on the ten-point scale.

Please tick your chosen score 1 = low 10 = high

	1	2	3	4	5	6	7	8	9	10
FLUENCY – speaks fluently and well										
CONFIDENCE – willing to accept alternative views, open to challenges, not defensive, able to be spontaneous										
PRESENCE – intensely alert to the present situation; shows gravitas; demonstrates stature and substance										
AUTHENTICITY – true to oneself; not putting on a front; reliable and dependable										
COURAGE – willing to be different; to challenge and question; think outside the box; take risks										
PASSION – shares personal values; energised; openly committed; enthusiastic; engages other people										
DEMEANOUR – upright physical bearing; well-turned out, always looks stylish and distinctive										

What do you think works well about how I come across to people?

....

....

What do you think works less well about how I come across to people? (Be honest, I will not get upset – promise!)

....

....

Please send this completed feedback to:

____

Analysing your rating

After receiving back completed questionnaires, here is what you do:

1 For each completed questionnaire, total the values shown by the ticks in each column. If a tick is in column 3, for example, this counts as three in your calculations.

The maximum score possible for each completed questionnaire is 70 (7 × 10).

2 Divide the score by 70 and multiply by 100, to arrive at their Charisma Rating for you.

Example:

Score: 45

Maximum possible 70

Charisma Rating = 45/70 × 100 = 64%

3 If five people completed the questionnaire, then combine all their scores and divide by that number:

Example:

Scores for 5 people: 200

Maximum possible: 350 (5 × 70)

Charisma Rating = 200/350 × 100 = 57%

Interpreting your Charisma Rating

Your best possible Charisma Rating is 100 per cent and it would be surprising if you achieved it; few people do.

Scores over 75 per cent suggest you have a strong charisma and should probably concentrate on building further on your particular strengths.

Scores under 75 per cent suggest you would benefit from working on selected areas of your charisma, including both strengths and weaknesses.

Next, review the answers to the two open-ended questions at the end. Can you identify any patterns or common themes in the various answers?

There is no single best way to achieve a strong Charisma Rating, for example, always smiling, having a noble bearing, giving eye contact, talking eloquently and so on. Instead, a good rating will stem from a unique blend of behaviours or traits. These are like colours on an artist's palette.

If you have a less than wonderful Charisma Profile there is no sense in punishing yourself. It is merely a device for answering important questions around aim and your charisma strengths and development needs.

Sharpen up your Charisma Aim

We can readily understand Charisma Aim. It is simply what you want to achieve through your presence. As we saw earlier, it is perfectly possible to 'switch on' and 'switch off' the use of your natural charisma. In making time for this book what exactly do you want to achieve, why does it matter to you? Similarly, in each interaction with other people, you will have a particular purpose and these matter too.

whatever aim you choose it should influence how you behave

Whatever aim you choose it should influence how you behave. The reaction you get from people may mean modifying your aim further in some way. Luckily, you also have some control over your behaviour and, if you are willing, you can even choose to alter it.

You are a one-off, a unique personality. If you attempt to act like Madonna, pretend to be Mandela, imitate Steve Jobs, or even copy your own boss to make an impact, you will probably crash and burn. This is why the A-B-C approach places a major focus on Being Yourself. You can simply adapt it to meet your particular needs in various situations.

If you cannot arrive at a vision or at least a basic Charisma Aim, it may partly explain why perhaps you make less impact than you deserve. For example, being unclear about what you want from a one-to-one meeting with your boss can send mixed messages and cause confusion.

For those occasions when you want to make a powerful and memorable impression, try to clarify:

Aim → Obstacles → Solutions

- Aim: what effect or result do I want to achieve?
- Obstacles: what might get in the way of achieving the aim?
- Solutions: how do I overcome these obstacles?

Sales people will recognise this sequence as part of discovering customer objections and finding ways to overcome them.

People with a strong charisma become skilled at identifying their communication aims, even when they do not always express it in these terms. Consciously or otherwise, they arrive at specific goals and then imagine how others will react to them. They select the messages and behaviours they believe will make them personally effective.

Your general Charisma Aim might be to impress people, get them to buy your service, make people listen to you with respect, raise your profile in the company and so on. However, these are not specific results. They need to be broken down further. For instance, the desired result from a forthcoming meeting might be:

- The customer signs on the dotted line of a contract.
- Everybody stands up and applauds.
- You receive a warm smiling handshake at the door.
- You win a commitment to start the project next Tuesday.
- You get the go-ahead to buy a new photocopier.
- At least ten volunteers come forward.
- The client agrees to meet again next month.
- You leave the session with at least five client prospects.

Notice the results do not express generalities but specific results. These are what you 'direct' your charisma to achieve. For this particular situation, this is what using your persona is about. By making the result so explicit, you make it easier to mobilise your charisma to make an impact.

It is also too easy to think of charisma as something you 'do' to people, rather than achieve a desired result.

Try the clarifying purpose exercise shown below. Obviously, you would not do this detailed analysis for every situation, only those where it is important to make a strong personal impact.

Clarifying your aim like this will make it easier to unleash your charisma and achieve the result you want.

Charisma purpose work out

In the empty table opposite,

- Write the name of a specific situation at work where you want to have a greater impact. It could be in a team meeting, talking with your boss, meeting a client, on the phone, or whatever.
- What is the specific result you want? Try to see it from the other person's point of view – what is in it for them?

- Describe what a 'win' would look like, sound like, and feel like.

Complete the table in as much detail as you can.

Situation	Specific result	What 'success' looks or feels like	Obstacles
Example: Our regular team meeting	Example: For people to listen to my ideas and take them seriously	Example: When I suggest something in our team meetings the other members actually talk about it, and I'd feel respected	Example: Tendency for people to feel free to interrupt
Now add your own example here:			

How clear is your intent? Could it be still clearer?

How might you deal with the obstacle (s)?

The above work out should help you describe what a successful charisma impact would look and feel like. Ask yourself, 'How would I recognise success?'

Try firming up your Charisma Aim by reducing it to the equivalent of a single newspaper headline, a one-line sentence that sums up what you want to achieve using your charisma.

An explicit Charisma Aim may seem far removed from the so-called 'magical' effect we associate with Extreme Charisma (see Chapter 1). Yet, in reality, those with Extreme Charisma usually know exactly what result they want and are uniquely resolved to achieve it.

Make a mental movie

Imagine you have a particular encounter you expect to have soon – to give a presentation to the top team, to meet a new client, to talk to your child's teacher at school.

Yet another useful tool is to devise a story, or mental movie of the exact outcome you want, with a beginning, middle and an end. Imagine it running like a movie in your head.

Suppose an email at work asks you to join an exciting new project and you want to win your manager's agreement. The mental movie might run something like this:

Beginning:

I smile as I enter the manager's office.

I sit down in the usual chair.

I feel relaxed.

Middle

She listens with interest.

I explain the project's benefits to her and the company and she keeps saying 'yes' lots of times.

When I see her smiling or nodding, I pop the question about a possible start date.

She readily agrees to a start date.

I smile with thanks.

End

I get up to leave, still smiling.

As I reach the door, I turn to say goodbye.

I see her smiling at me.

Do not worry if this feels an unlikely scenario – for example, in reality your manager hardly ever smiles, or spends too little time listening or showing interest.

Simply keep running this mental movie in your head, imagining the ideal outcome you want. See it running in black and white, in technicolour, as a silent movie, as a fly-on-the-wall documentary. Even 'watch it' at times when you are really in the room with the manager.

You do not need to be a particularly visual person to create these kinds of mental scenes. You simply daydream! Allow your mind gently to construct the story in bits and pieces, until something emerges, describing what you want to happen.

The more you play with the mental scenario, the more you can adjust it so that your charisma works harder to produce it. Your charisma is not a separate part of you, but needs to integrate with whatever you are trying to achieve. The mental movie is one way to help that occur.

Constantly visualising your Charisma Aim may seem rather fanciful but there is credible research showing that these mental exercises can actually influence reality. The movie you keep running in your head can directly influence how you behave, including your body language and therefore ultimately your Charisma Effect.

Until you have tried it, please hold back from dismissing this mental movie and its power to help you make a stronger personal impact. It really works!

Tackle multiple aims

In the earlier exercise to clarify your personal impact aim, you chose just one headline to analyse in detail. In real life, of course, you may be juggling with several entirely different headlines. For example, you might want your charisma to achieve a stronger impact on your boss, raise your profile in your team, build a long-term relationship with a client, and gain agreement from a colleague for something.

While multiple aims can be compatible, they may also make it hard to focus your charisma energies. Trying to achieve them all simultaneously may dilute rather than strengthen your charisma impact.

Since multiple Charisma Aims can be distracting, try to prioritise them:

1 List each of your Charisma Aims.
2 Rank each in terms of importance from highest to lowest.
3 Select the highest-ranking aim to tackle first and do the second highest one next, and so on.

Charisma aims	Ranking (1 = high)
More impact with boss	2
Higher profile in the team	3
Build relationship with client	1
Agreement for new project	4

'I always wanted to be somebody, but now I realise I should have been more specific.'

Lily Tomalin, actor

Part 2

Be yourself

The seven essential charisma behaviours

This next part of our A-B-C approach to developing your charisma deals with seven essential behaviours:

- fluency
- confidence
- presence
- authenticity
- courage
- passion
- demeanour.

This part offers ways to adjust and develop these behaviours, so you become more effective in your interactions and make the impression you want.

Chapter 3

Fluency

'I want that glib and oily art', demands Cordelia in Shakespeare's *King Lear* after realising she is not being persuasive enough. People with strong charisma tend to be articulate, and whether you call it oily art or the ability to talk well, personal success within, and often outside, many organisations usually demands a certain way with words.

being fluent at work is now almost mandatory

This is not solely about public speaking – though this may be important – being fluent at work is now almost mandatory. To enhance your charisma you may need to develop your facility with words, phrases, ideas, values, issues, feelings and general communication.

Since communication is a two-way affair, what you transmit also needs to be received by the other person. You will only be fully articulate when those on the receiving end absorb your message.

- If they haven't heard it, you haven't said it.
- Read: make yourself encounter words you do not already know and find out what they mean by reading well-written books that challenge your vocabulary.
- Take classes: explore subjects like art, music, theatre, literature, languages, philosophy, science and psychology that offer new ways of looking at and expressing ideas.

- Listen: take every opportunity to listen to individuals who express themselves well – avoid relying on politicians, athletes and other celebrities, most of whom parrot trite phrases.
- Conversation: find ways to get involved in thoughtful, mentally challenging conversations.

Explain complicated ideas simply

'Great leaders are almost always great simplifiers, who can cut through argument, debate and doubt to offer a solution everybody can understand', commented US General Colin Powell. Because the average human attention span lasts just 15 seconds or less, we need to learn to get our messages across quickly. Almost anyone can make a subject complicated, even how to make a good cup of tea – the official UK guidance on this runs to six pages!

almost anyone can make a subject complicated, even how to make a good cup of tea

People with a strong Charisma Effect realise the importance of reducing complexity and ruthlessly simplifying their message so what they say lands easily. For instance, few people really understand biotechnology but that does not prevent the best scientists, such as leading theoretical physicist, futurist and TV presenter Dr Michio Kaku, from talking about it so most of us can broadly understand what is involved.

Some of the worst anti-simplicity offenders tend to be highly committed professionals who thrive on, and even reward, obscurity. With this in mind, financial services company ING Direct deliberately recruits non-bankers able to challenge the status quo. It recognises that familiarity leads to myopia and subject-matter experts who rarely view things the way customers do.

Simplifying complicated ideas means giving jargon its marching orders. While jargon can be a useful shorthand between fellow professionals, it may also reduce personal impact, even among knowledgeable colleagues.

- Avoid jargon if you want to simplify.

Another way of simplifying is to explain the 'big idea'. You cut through technical complexity to show what lies behind an issue or problem. The film director Cecil B. DeMille once summed up his proposed blockbuster film of Samson and Delilah for Paramount officials as: 'Boy meets girl – and what a boy, and what a girl!'

For a while, super simplification conquered Hollywood and everyone pitching ideas for a movie was expected to do it in a few words or sentences.

- Girl meets girl and they drive off a cliff.
- Martians conquer the world but die from a virus.
- A sweet little fish loses its parents and finds them again.

Try the simplification work out overleaf.

Communicate convincingly

When the government's chief scientist sits opposite the UK's prime minister and says the country needs to expand its use of nuclear power, he carries more weight as an independent adviser than, say, the head of British Nuclear Fuels Ltd pushing for exactly the same thing. However, being convincing only partly relies on your role or job. Studies of successful leaders in highly profitable companies confirm that many of them do not have a particularly strong charisma, yet they still manage to sound convincing.

Simplification work out

Just for fun, and because it will help you practise aiming for the big idea, see how many of the following films you can explain in one short sentence.

Film	**Explanation**
The Matrix	
Lord of the Rings (any one film)	
The Godfather	
Pulp Fiction	
Jaws	
The Terminator	
Alien	
Fight Club	
Wuthering Heights	
Pretty Woman	

Alternatively, choose half a dozen films you know well and use them to write your one-line summary.

Conviction

When people share their passion or enthusiasm for something it is catching and helps convince people. Tap into your own conviction by starting with what excites or interests you about your message.

If you are unconvinced by what you want to say, why should others be the opposite? Try breaking your message into smaller parts to see if you can uncover some aspect of it that fully ignites your interest or enthusiasm. For example, suppose you must talk to customers about your company's new product yet you feel unenthusiastic about it. Rather than hoping for the best, find some aspect about this product, no matter how small, that you do see as interesting or convincing and focus on that.

- To convince others, first convince yourself.

Content

Although actual words are a minor part of sounding convincing, the contents of your verbal messages can potentially affect credibility.

- Do you present enough facts to support your case?
- Is what you say logical and easy to follow?
- Is the content sufficiently brief for people to absorb it?

For example, in a job interview, to avoid sounding merely boastful, can you support your previous experience with solid evidence? Are there examples, statistics, expert references or even testimonials to support your case? Or when discussing some issue with your boss, do you always include solid facts to support what you say, rather than mainly relying on assertion? In a team meeting, underpin your opinions with facts and tangible evidence. Beefing up your content in this way may mean more time on preparation than you currently allow, but inadequate preparation tends to be a killer, especially with formal presentations.

underpin your opinions with facts and tangible evidence

Being logical and easy to follow will strengthen your impact on others. Not only are most people's attention spans short, people can usually only remember two or three points made during a verbal interchange. For instance, the actual order in which you present information matters.

- A foundation stone for sounding convincing is to give people the most important information first.

Bring your message to life

Fluent people often enliven their impact using creative phrases. 'We're still dancing', claimed Chuck Prince as head of Citibank when talking about possible board differences. A memorable visual image can be an important part of building one's Charisma Effect.

Claiming that the seemingly impossible is possible – namely a better world – Professor Hans Rosling ends his now famous presentation at the TED conference, seen by over 500,000 people over the internet, by swallowing a large steel sword (visit www.gapminder.org).

Metaphors and similes

Metaphors and similes paint memorable pictures in people's minds, describing something as *if* it were something else. They help explain conceptual ideas, convey complex notions and provide a shared understanding, allowing us to use verbal shorthand. Example metaphors are:

- 'This family has rock-solid values.'
- 'There are a few rotten apples in that team.'
- 'We've got to bust the speed limit on this one.'

You may associate metaphors with poetry, literature and art, yet we all use them, often unconsciously, during daily conversation. Because they are so effective at quickly conveying tangible and conceptual information they are woven into the fabric of our English language. When Chief Executive Lee Iacocca was trying to rescue Chrysler he carefully did not ask the US government for a 'rescue package' but instead talked about a 'safety net' to prevent the company having to fire many people.

Similes use 'as' or 'like' to compare something to something else, for example:

- 'He's as hard as nails.'
- 'She's as tough as old boots.'
- 'Turns up here on Tuesdays like clockwork.'

If you have an idea or a message you want to get across to colleagues, try choosing an object or an action that is completely unrelated. For example, suppose you want to sell your team the idea of a new activity, and also enjoy whitewater rafting – what connections can you make between the two? Making them, however tenuous, may produce some memorable and persuasive phrases.

Speak clearly and audibly

We are so used to hearing our own voice that we tend to pay little attention to how we sound when we speak. This is because we have lots of casual, low-level communication and mainly get by. Our friends seem to understand us easily and accept who we are and how we sound, but to achieve the Charisma Effect requires attention to what we say and how we say it, and that includes:

- diction – whether you pronounce words and sentences clearly or not
- pitch – how high or low your voice goes
- volume – whether or not you can be heard
- tone – what mood your voice conveys, such as friendliness, anger, etc.
- pace – how fast you speak.

Diction

One reason why people do not speak clearly is that they are not carefully checking that their message is landing, which is why eye contact can actually help with diction.

> eye contact can actually help with diction

Check if you speak clearly by being brave enough to obtain feedback. One way is to record yourself speaking and listen with a critical ear for whether or not your speech is clear, crisp and easy to follow. Alternatively, during a conversation you might ask if the other person finds you speak clearly. This may be a bit daunting but it will give you the information you need.

You can also try these ideas.

- Watch yourself talking in the mirror – what are your first impressions of your speaking voice?
- Practise enunciating your words. Demosthenes the Greek orator improved his clarity of speech by putting a pebble in his mouth until he could be understood, despite its presence. Rather than risk swallowing a pebble, try placing a pencil horizontally in your mouth to force you to enunciate your words more clearly. (Be careful not to choke on it though!)
- Practise talking more slowly. Giving your words an extra second or two to leave your mouth can really help with your personal impact. Pausing also works because it allows your listener to digest what you have said (see also page 53).

Speaking clearly is so important that, while you can certainly tackle this on your own, it may also be helpful to spend some time with a specialist voice coach.

Voice work out

1 Smile broadly while you read the paragraph below:

'This team is doing really well, we have surpassed all our targets and are on track for a record-breaking month. Well done!'

2 Now read the same paragraph while you frown and tighten your jaw.

3 Note how your facial expression changed the sound of the message.

Pitch

People with weak charisma are often unaware that they talk in a monotone. Boring voices occur for several fairly common reasons: dreary content, over-reliance on a written script and a voice pitch that sounds wooden – that is, unmusical.

Reading your presentation aloud is a guaranteed way to sound dull and reduces your voice to a charisma-sapping drone. Even great actors find it challenging to speak an entire script and make it sound interesting.

To vary your pitch, make sure you move your body. It works! Other ways include the following:

- Breathe more deeply, and relax.
- 'Lean' on important words and phrases, putting energy into them.
- Inject more emotion into what you say.
- Emphasise the ends of statements and questions.

Again this is a tricky area of personal development where a qualified voice coach can quickly help you to achieve a more varied and interesting delivery.

Volume

Entrepreneur Karen Darby, a big personality who sold her price comparison website SimplySwitch for £22 million, speaks 'like she is making sure she reaches the cheap seats, even though there are just two of us sitting in the small room', commented *The Guardian* in October 2007. In contrast, Dorothy Parker, the famous US writer and humorist, deliberately spoke so quietly that to catch her words people had to lean towards her. They were rewarded with brilliant satirical wit that generated her particular impact. In choosing to talk so quietly, she knew exactly what she was doing, projecting just enough to hold people's attention.

talking either too loudly or too quietly can undermine your Charisma Effect

Talking either too loudly or too quietly can undermine your Charisma Effect, so it is worth checking out if you currently have the volume control too high or low. Do people often ask you to speak up or repeat yourself? If they do, it probably indicates you have rather a quiet voice, even though it may sound perfectly normal to you.

Strengthen your voice work out

1 Stand up straight. This enables your lungs to expand to their full capacity and your diaphragm to be unrestricted.
2 Take a deep breath and fill up your lungs.
3 Speak as though the air is coming from your stomach.
4 Speak evenly, not letting all the air go into one phrase and resulting in a wild yell. Having taken a nice deep breath, you will have the benefit of plenty of air to sustain you through an entire steady sentence.

It takes a while to perfect the technique so give yourself plenty of practice.

If you are worried you might suffer from a strident or harsh voice, watch for signs such as people withdrawing from you, even if only slightly, or perhaps wincing as you talk. Alternatively, be brave and ask some trusted colleagues for direct feedback.

Using loudness work out

1 Speak each of the following sentences softly.

- I didn't say that!
- Leave me alone.
- Give it to me.
- Get out of here.
- I want it now.

2 Then using the size values of each word in the sentence as a guide, increase volume with word size.

- I didn't say that.
- Leave me alone.
- Give it to me.
- Get out of here.
- I want it now.

Note how the meaning of what you say changes with the volume.

Tone

Tone conveys whether you are being friendly, angry, cheerful, patient, etc. and can play an important part in establishing your personal impact.

No matter how relaxed he tried to appear, ex UK prime minister John Major's public voice always sounded alien and strangulated. It is hard to appear cheerful, confident or persuasive if your voice says to your listeners, 'Can you hear how tense I am?'

To create a rich, creamy tone involves using your diaphragm, your vocal cords and the amount of sound resonating in your throat, mouth and head. I know it sounds a bit complicated, which is why having training from a voice expert can really help.

For a simple tone work out, try the one shown below. If you feel it does not help, consider looking for some outside support. This might include visiting a qualified voice coach, someone with a professional qualification in this area. A good voice coach can show you ways to vary your tone so your speech sounds more musical and attractive.

Tone work out

1. Hum lightly and continuously.
2. Place your hand gently around your neck – as if your hand was a tie.
3. Feel all the muscles in your neck and under your jaw relax.
4. Say 'umm-hmm' in your natural speaking voice. You should feel a vibration in your face and under your hand on your neck. Feel how easily the 'hmm' part of umm-hmm comes out.
5. Now, speak with that same easy hum in your voice. Keep the sense of an easy hum in the front of your face. Don't push. Let your speaking voice grow out of that easy hum. If you lose the hum, you lose your breath connection.
6. Relax your upper body, including your shoulders, neck and abdominal muscles, and your voice will sound gentler and more pleasant.

Pace

Fast-talking used-car sales people, politicians and lawyers shoot out their words like bullets. Slow talkers drag them out so you end up hanging on their words. Both types of speakers attempt to use speed to exert control over their listeners and hopefully increase their impact.

Normal conversational speech occurs in rapid bursts of sound, which is why talking more slowly can often be so effective in building your Charisma Effect. Ways to slow down include:

- add more pauses to give people time to think
- vary your delivery pace, so sometimes you slow down and at other times speed up
- use less energy in actually speaking, so words come out more smoothly and less jerkily.

If you think you talk too slowly, first check this out with colleagues since it could in fact be a great asset.

Ways to speed up your speech include:

- put more energy into actually talking so the words come out more explosively
- use verbal exercises to limber up before talking – professional actors and presenters nearly always do this as part of their preparation
- read aloud a list of some kind and time yourself with a stop watch. Practise until you read the list at faster and faster speeds.

Use silence appropriately

Those who generate strong charisma soon realise they can use silence in a positive way by leaving space for reflection and for others to fill in the gaps. As US humorist Josh Billings put it: ‘Silence is one of the hardest arguments to refute.’

> silence can create a feeling of openness and spaciousness

Silence can create a feeling of openness and spaciousness for yourself and others. It can also add gravitas to how you come across. You allow people time to think when you do not rush to fill silences left by others, and offer them a silent form of respect.

An entirely different kind of silence can damage your charisma by making you appear aggressive, unresponsive or simply unfriendly. Can you think of a time when you used silence as a weapon – perhaps after an argument with a friend or loved one? Once you become aware of what you are doing it becomes easier to tackle it. Gradually, as you become more vigilant the pattern will weaken. So work on the following:

- Become aware of your own silence.
- Sharpen your awareness of your own reaction to silence.
- Work at becoming comfortable with silence.
- Use silence in a positive, not negative, way.

Silence work out

1 Phone a friend and say you want to do an experiment.
2 Explain you are both going to look at your watches and stay silent for a full 15 seconds. Try it. You both know what the plan is and yet you will be surprised at how hard it is to stay silent.
3 Next, try the same thing face to face, this time for a whole minute. What were your feelings about the experience? When did you begin to feel uncomfortable? What were the signs of discomfort? Were you able to look at the other person during the silence or did you find yourself avoiding their gaze after a while? Did you smile, laugh or make nervous noises during the silence test?
4 Try giving yourself permission to use silence for a specific purpose – for example, to make an impact in a conversation or to get feedback.

When you use silence well, you will tend to be more observant and focused. Positive silence means your mind does not function like a high-rev motor, remaining instead quiet and still. Those around you soon absorb this calmness and respond.

Silence also works well in silencing others. For example, if someone keeps chattering at you, leaving you little or no air time, you can use silence to bring this to a natural and painless end. You simply withhold encouragement through lack of positive responses such as nods, facial expressions and other kinds of verbal reinforcement. Faced with such a blank canvas the average person tends to stop talking, falling silent themselves within about two minutes.

Managers able to sit comfortably with silence in a positive way build their personal impact and make space for others to talk. They can draw out information that otherwise would not become known – for example, confronting a poorly performing member of staff or one accused of a misdemeanour.

When you use silence well you gain the power of the pause. A pause in the right place at the right time gives you time to breathe, time to consider what it is you're going to say next, time to receive and digest the feedback you're getting from your audience.

Leaders who communicate well usually listen hard for the silences of the people they are addressing. They detect enthusiastic agreement, bitter resistance or unspoken misgivings. This comes from focusing, really listening and staying present (see Chapter 5). When this happens, the leader can often achieve strong charisma, often without saying anything at all.

> *'Somebody's boring me. I think it's me.'*
>
> Dylan Thomas, poet, author and playwright

Chapter 4
Confidence

‘If you don’t think you’re wonderful, why should anyone else?’ asked the wisecracking actress Mae West. Her legendary self-assurance did not just happen, she really worked at it.

Anthony Howard, one of Britain’s most distinguished and best-known political observers, regularly appeared on television. He had a famously unusual, some would say ugly, face yet his confidence soon made you forget his looks; as he talked, his personal impact soon became apparent.

> self-confidence plays a vital role in creating charisma

Self-confidence plays a vital role in creating charisma and ‘is the first requisite to great undertakings’ argued Samuel Johnson, one of England’s most brilliant yet notoriously ugly individuals.

Confidence conveys power; power to influence and affect people’s thoughts, feelings and behaviour. Exude it and you will be more likely to make the kind of impact you want than if people see a lack of self-assurance.

Even Winston Churchill was not always entirely sure of himself and complained bitterly to his wife Clementine that, despite being prime minister, he felt inadequate and without a strong impact when dealing with important people and particular actors on the world stage. In his case, he was such a powerful figure that his Charisma Effect and his audiences’ expectations helped disguise his occasional lapses in confidence.

Occasionally there is a difference between the internal confidence you possess and the external confidence you convey to others. For example, even the best stage actors may admit to internal doubts and lack of self-assurance when tackling important roles, yet once they appear on stage you would never know they are so uncertain.

But more often there is a strong link between internal confidence and the external results other people interpret as self-assurance. As one commentator puts it: 'If you think you have confidence you do, and if you don't think you have got it, even if you have it, you don't have it.'

Sustained confidence comes from practice, leading to some new ability (competence), which in turn makes you more sure of yourself (confidence):

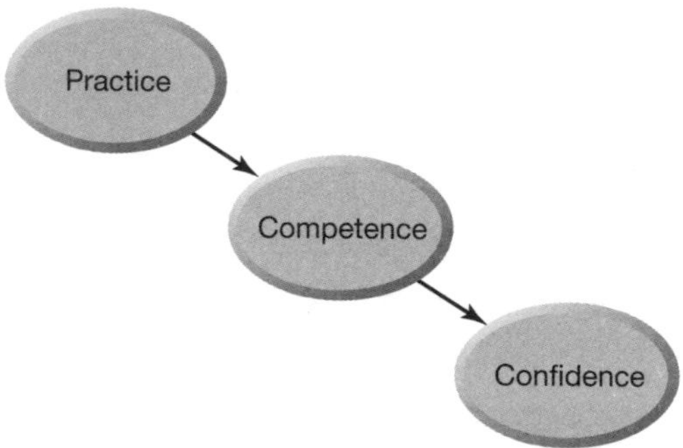

Confident behaviour shows itself in posture and other less obvious aspects of your behaviour, such as subtle body language signals. For example, other people experience you as:

- being relaxed, rather than rigid
- being flexible, with a wide-ranging voice and movement
- being in control – your movements are not shaky or awkward
- having a clear intention.

You can practise all of these – for example, getting clearer about your intention or becoming more aware about your body language. Also check out Chapter 9 on demeanour.

Confidence builders

- Intent: develop a strong, clear intention about the effect you want to achieve and stay fully conscious of it.
- Relax: create an open body posture suggesting you are ready for anything.
- Voice: cultivate a pleasant voice with variations that also conveys assuredness.
- Open-ended questions: use these to involve other people and avoid the more limited yes or no answer; then follow these up with appropriate comments and more questions.
- You-statements: these directly address the other person – not in an accusatory way but one that signals a direct and personalised focus on the other person – for example, 'Do you agree?', 'How do you feel about that?'
- Avoid powerless language: steer clear of statements that express a lack of conviction, make you sound like a victim (see Chapter 2) or seem unduly self-critical.
- Be proactive: take the initiative in the conversation process; introduce issues or views that allow others to make a contribution.
- Look people in the eye and maintain eye contact long enough to send a clear message: 'I am confident, I am interested in you.'

Act as if

Behave as if others are happy to see you and they are more likely to feel that way. Act as if people want to hear what you have to say and they will

> act as if people want to hear what you have to say

tend to do so. Act as if they respect you and they are more willing to treat you accordingly. Eventually it no longer becomes an act.

The 'act as if' principle requires you to invest most of your attention on the other person, or members of the group. Rather than wasting energy dealing with internal self-doubt you simply refuse to give it house room.

Behave like a victim and, sure enough, that is how people will experience you. Assume people will ignore you, then that is exactly what will happen. With charisma it always comes down to a choice – 'What is my intent?'

- **People will assume about you what you assume about yourself:** Your attitudes bounce back to you from other people. For example, if you think members of your team will probably ignore you, eventually the team will agree with you. If you think you have no opinions, then people will start seeing you as someone with nothing to say. Think of yourself as charming, intelligent and someone of substance, and sure enough that is how eventually you will be perceived.
- **People will tend to mirror back your present emotional state:** If you are enthusiastic others will tend to become enthusiastic too; if you are unhappy about being in the room with people, they will feel that way about you too; if you are interested in people, they will tend to be interested in you.
- **Expectations about how people will behave affect their actual behaviour:** If you think your boss hates you, chances are they will end up doing just that; if you do not expect people to sit up and take notice when you arrive, they will get the message and respond accordingly.

How does this self-fulfilling process work? Are people reading your mind, or what? To some extent they do just that, but not using telepathy. Instead they read the many deliberate and hidden messages given out through your bearing, your facial expression, your gestures and other body language. When you 'act as if', you cannot help sending out the positive messages that make an impact.

Scenarios

These mental gymnastics can also influence how you approach communication challenges: from speaking at conferences to entering a room full of strangers, from meeting your boss to raising an issue in a team meeting. You imagine a whole experience to suit the occasion. Here are three different scenarios.

1 **Be a party host:** You imagine everyone you encounter in an event is a guest at your party, paying particular attention to each person before moving on to the next. This is a great confidence builder because you certainly have the right to be at your own party!
2 **Be curious:** Focus on a target such as being curious about why people have chosen to attend a meeting. Equally, you could choose to be curious about their views on some issue or if they have blue eyes. It hardly matters, so long as you give yourself a curiosity target to work on. This externalises your thoughts and establishes communication.
3 **Message giver:** You approach every encounter as creating a unique opportunity to convey your important message. You talk to people as if they are keen to hear your message.

Emotional intelligence

Emotional intelligence (or EI) is being aware about what is happening to others emotionally and at the same time knowing how your own emotions are affected. For example, low emotional intelligence would be not realising that you make others feel devalued, inadequate, intimidated, angry, frustrated or guilty.

While there is some debate about how far one can increase ordinary intelligence, you can certainly develop your emotional intelligence. What sets emotional intelligence apart from ordinary people skills is the ability to read the social dynamic – or what is happening at any moment during an interaction.

Developing your emotional intelligence means you also become socially aware and this can generate personal magnetism. Having a magnetic personality is therefore potentially within the reach of all of us. You attract people because they experience you as intensely aware of them – in showbiz terms, it is the audience that counts, not oneself.

Emotional intelligence is like a special radar for reading situations and interpreting the behaviours of others, their intentions, emotional states and willingness to interact. The trouble is, we sometimes suffer from radar blind spots where we either misread a situation or do not read it at all. For example, if you feel free to walk over to someone and immediately launch into saying how terrific your company is, regardless of whether they are ready to hear about it, then you have failed to read the radar correctly. Or if you say something that completely upsets another person and do not even realise it, then again your radar has failed.

emotional intelligence is like a special radar

Ways to increase your emotional intelligence

Other chapters deal with aspects of improving your emotional intelligence, in particular those on aim (Chapter 2), authenticity (Chapter 6) and presence (Chapter 5). Here we will focus on situational awareness, being able to 'read' the situational radar screen.

Useful tools to help you read the situation include the following:

- Space – what is the spatial picture in this situation?
- Behaviours – what do you observe in this situation?
- Advanced sensory activity – what is happening in this situation?

Space

Human beings inhabit a space and you can read a lot from how they choose to do that. For example, when you attend your next meeting, as you enter, look around at how people have chosen to spread themselves out, or not, whether they are leaning inwards or outwards, and what other signals you can pick up from the spatial picture before you.

Does the spatial arrangement seem businesslike, tranquil, alert, strained or part of a ritual? Do people look comfortable or ill at ease? Does the picture seem welcoming or not? Who sits where and why – for example, does the most senior person always sit at the head of the table? Where would it be best to place yourself in this picture and why?

Next time you enter someone's office, take a closer look at the spatial arrangements. Do they seem designed to emphasise the occupant's power? Do they promote or deter communication, or encourage or discourage any intimacy? What else can you read from the spatial arrangements?

Behaviours

When you apply emotional intelligence you observe closely other people's behaviour and consciously look for non-verbal information about the situation, including body postures, movements, gestures, facial expressions, pitch and tone of voice. These behaviours can signal all sorts of messages that once spotted you must then try to make sense of. For example, how do people in the room signal deference or authority, who touches whom, or enters the room first or last?

Try watching the TV or a film with the sound off and observe how people move and communicate without words. This kind of observation is what experienced poker players often rely on to 'read' their opponents.

Advanced sensory activity – what is happening?

This goes beyond overt behaviours and involves being alert to far less obvious factors that may tell you how people are feeling and what they are thinking. For example, watch people's breathing – are they taking shallow or deep breaths, breathing rapidly or apparently calmly?

check out involuntary signs such as the pallor of people's skin

Check out involuntary signs such as the pallor of people's skin. What is this telling you about what is happening inside the person? For example, if someone looks flushed is it a signal of disagreement, anger or perhaps embarrassment?

Finally, assess people's energy levels – are they high or low, rising or falling? Signs of changing energy levels may stem from many sources such as body posture, eye contact, hand or foot movements and so on.

> *'Even if you're in a situation where you feel uncomfortable or out of place, don't try to swim against the current. Change direction. Find the flow and follow it.'*
>
> Oprah Winfrey, television presenter

Charisma generally goes hand-in-hand with confidence. It is hard to imagine someone with charisma who does not also exude a high degree of confidence, yet the two attributes are not identical. Just because you are confident does not mean you automatically acquire a powerful charisma. Equally, those with charisma may struggle to fully integrate confidence into their lives. Insecurity may lurk in the background like a black cloud, as it did with Marilyn Monroe for example.

Despite a strong charisma, many people find their normally cast-iron self-certainty occasionally takes a dive. Actress Winona Ryder admitted to depression after splitting up with ex-fiancé Johnny Depp, who himself has suffered from anxiety disorder. Others with confidence-sapping mental states include Anthony Hopkins, Hugh Laurie, Catherine Zeta-Jones, J.K. Rowling, Mel Gibson, Jim Carrey and Cher.

The power of genuine confidence is that when you exude it you automatically transmit positive emotions to other people. They quickly detect your state of mind and unconsciously find themselves mirroring it back to you. It becomes a mutually reinforcing process, leaving everyone feeling better. Leaving people feeling better is an essential requirement of charisma.

You build self-confidence through practice. You may posses a super-high IQ, a gift for witty banter or stunning good looks, yet you may still not be bursting with self-confidence. Confidence has many facets, and you will need to explore what builds and what undermines yours.

You are more than your personality, your body, or your mind. You are part of a world of ever-changing opportunities and situations. If, in enhancing your charisma, confidence seems an issue for you, invest time in exploring some of the ways described here for moving it onto a firmer base. Use each situation where you feel a low level of confidence as a useful platform from which to change direction and try something new.

Chapter 5

Presence

In the film *All That Jazz*, the main character starts each day by staring intensely into a mirror. Drawing himself up and with a determined, if world-weary air, he announces aloud: 'It's Show time!' It's his way of becoming present, of raising his state of awareness, of switching himself 'on'.

While you may not need to remind yourself daily that it is show time, you do need to find your own way of triggering your presence. It's an essential part of building your charisma.

Presence demands your energy and is literally being entirely in the 'here and now.' It mainly takes two forms:

> presence is literally being entirely in the 'here and now'

- Being super-alert to your surroundings.
- Having highly tuned sensory awareness.

This kind of alertness has a considerable impact on those coming into contact with it. It also explains why, when these two behaviours are operating at full power, Extreme Charisma can seem so awesome and even unattainable.

Yet you do not need Extreme Charisma to create presence. Plenty of people do this through adopting less demanding versions of the two above behaviours.

Take for example Peter, who provides IT recruitment services for the clients of his consultancy. In a small group of strangers, he seems fully aware of what is going on around him and chats to people without inhibition, smiling warmly at each, making excellent eye contact. When faintly rebuffed by one person, he moves without resentment to the next and soon emerges as the life and soul of the group. When everyone goes their separate ways, most, if not all, will recall him with amusement and pleasure.

Peter can mobilise his presence even if it is not as high octane as the extreme kind. His natural presence is always available when he needs it, and he is entirely at home with himself, knows who he is and what really matters to him.

In your journey towards a stronger charisma, explore your relationship to presence and build your awareness of it still further. Try the Presence work out below.

Presence work out

1 Sit fully upright in your chair, alert, relaxed and looking forward.
2 Become aware of your breathing – focus on your body moving the air in and out, in and out.
3 Slow your breath down slightly by pausing five seconds on an intake of air, then let go and push the air out as if sending it down to your feet. Do this at least five times.
4 Without moving your head or eyes, start noticing what reaches your peripheral vision – the outside edges of your sight.
5 Pay close attention to the sounds around you. Listen for what seems near and far, loud and soft, high and low, regular or sporadic.
6 Sniff the air gently three or four times. What does the air taste like? Are there are particular smells you notice? If you are wearing perfume or aftershave, try to detect it.

7 Move your attention to your body, try to become aware of the sensation caused by your socks or stockings, or footwear. Can you feel the weight of your body pressing down into the chair?

8 Experience fully this moment when life seems to slow down, and immediate pressures recede to create a new awareness.

9 Finally, start letting go of the intensity of being present, relaxing into a more familiar state of being.

When you are fully present you are both alert to your surroundings and acutely conscious of atmosphere, hidden tensions, expectations, even perhaps what people are thinking.

> A small village in central Europe invited a rabbi famous for his wisdom to visit. For weeks the local Jewish population debated what matters of great import they should raise with him, what conflicts they wanted him to resolve, and what advice to ask for.
>
> When finally the rabbi arrived, he entered the room where everyone had gathered to welcome him. He stood there silently for a while, becoming fully present while everyone waited expectantly for his first words. Instead the rabbi began to dance. He danced and danced and soon everyone was dancing too, until exhausted they came to a complete standstill.
>
> In the panting silence that followed, the smiling rabbi looked around, smiled and enquired: 'Any more questions?'

The impact of presence can cause you to be seen, heard, noticed, respected and acknowledged. Of the many ways to increase your presence, you might find it helpful to use: the presence highway code; two kinds of energy; being spirited; raising your self-awareness.

The presence highway code

This works particularly well just before interacting with people and especially in formal presenting situations. The code requires you to:

- Stop
- Breathe
- Look
- Listen
- Feel.

These actions make you more alert, raise your awareness of your environment, and boost your presence. (See the box below.)

The presence highway code

Stop: Slow down and do not rush to start speaking. The pause gives precious moments 'to arrive' both mentally and emotionally. If you're anxious, it allows your body time to adjust and for those butterflies in your stomach to start flying in formation.

Breathe: Gently take a few deep breaths, without heaving your chest or raising your shoulders. At the top of your intake of breath hold it, and count slowly to five. Doing this several times will slow your heart beat, reducing the discharge of adrenaline into your system which causes feelings of anxiety or excitement.

Look: In a small group make eye contact with each person, just briefly, before starting to talk. The effect of silence and demanding visual connection can be amazing and convey unmistakeable presence. In a large group, look for a familiar or friendly face. Continue making eye contact with a few chosen individuals across the entire audience.

While looking, ask yourself, 'What do I observe right now?' and hear the answers in your head as you continue without speaking.

For example you may notice people smiling, frowning, looking distracted, fiddling with phones or shuffling papers. What is this telling you about the state of readiness of your audience?

Listen: For sounds that convey something useful about the people with whom you are about to communicate. Are they restless; is there a stillness yet, suggesting they are ready for you to begin?

Feel: Use all your senses, including your natural intuition to detect what is happening around you. Give all senses full rein to uncover subtle signs that might suggest how best to communicate at this moment.

Mark Twain, the US humorist and author, once started a lecture by silently contemplating his waiting audience for an extended period. He studied the auditorium as if wanting to look every single person in the eye. After nearly 10 minutes of extraordinary silence, the entire audience spontaneously broke into applause.

Twain was using an extreme version of the speaker's presence highway code. He was getting in touch with his audience, making contact at a deep level and being utterly present.

Use two kinds of energy

Watch someone with an obvious presence and even when sitting entirely still they appear energised. They are drawing upon two separate sources of power. The first stems from physicality, the alertness of the entire body for whatever will happen next, drawing energy from the outside world. The other energy used comes from within. You can tap this source of power through bringing your whole person to the situation – who you are, your values and knowing yourself. Though this sounds mystical or metaphysical, in fact you are permitting the mask to drop, so people see the individual behind it.

Here are some practical ways to draw on the energy within you.

- Give yourself permission to feel and be vulnerable. Rather than fighting tension or anxiety, tell yourself it is safe to open yourself to this person or these people.
- Think of being in a castle, lowering the drawbridge and stepping out with a gesture of welcome.
- Consciously slow down your rate of breathing (see the presence highway code earlier).
- Rather than just glancing at people, put definite energy into making eye contact, and into your facial expressions and body language. In making connections you do not do anything violent or jerky, merely act more deliberately.
- Remind yourself of your personal values and their relationship to the particular moment. If you are unsure what your personal values are, try the Values work out below.

Values work out

Becoming clear about what your personal values are can help to raise your self-awareness, feed your inner expression of energy and strengthen your presence.

1 List what you value or what matters most in your life. What do you feel really passionate about? Take time to think about this.

....

....

....

....

2 Think about how you put values into action in your life.

3 Suggest ways in which these values show up in your daily existence.

....

....

....

....

4 Choose one personal value you feel most strongly about. Would people you know well know this about you?

Show the results to a close friend or family member. Do they recognise you from seeing what you have produced? How do these values affect you at work?

Example

1 What do I value most; what am I passionate about?

The environment, justice, my marriage, being creative, my health.

2 How do I put these values into action in my daily life?

Cycle to work; active in local conservation groups; belong to Amnesty International, maintain a good work/life balance; always trying out new ideas; work out weekly; vegetarian.

Energised people with a clear positive message can create a strong presence and be extremely persuasive. Somehow, anything seems possible and all obstacles appear to be surmountable.

Be spirited

You sometimes see the lack of spirit on the football pitch, in tennis matches and other competitive situations. Heads droop, bodies flag, despondency prevails and it is not always due to running out of energy. Sometimes it is just a lack of any will to continue.

Spirited people can be magnetic; others usually like being with them because their presence vibrates with life. To experience you as spirited, people need to see you as lively, positive and animated. Smiling, laughing, expressing optimism, eyes wide and alert, body posture all contribute to conveying spirit.

> part of being spirited arises from your use of energy

Part of being spirited arises from your use of energy. Actors, for example, despite feeling low or even demoralised, learn to draw on reserves of energy to lift their spirits just before they go on stage. You may need to do the same by paying special attention to whether or not you are fully using your energy.

Raise your self-awareness

This theme runs throughout the journey towards enhancing your Charisma Effect. Ways to deliberately increase your self-awareness include exploring the self that you hide from people, listening and trusting your intuition and connecting with people who inspire you.

Self-awareness includes discovering how your own behaviour may be actually reducing your Charisma Effect.

Explore your hidden aspects

What really lies behind your mask? If you seldom take a long look, it can be challenging to explore the hidden and perhaps uncomfortable parts of yourself. Why bother? Surely if you have tucked away part of yourself it must be for a good reason? That may be true, but if these hidden parts either reduce your Charisma Effect or could be used to enhance it, then exploring them could be extremely worthwhile.

'Well, what is my hidden self?' you may ask. While of course only you can answer that, otherwise it wouldn't be hidden, it is most likely to consist of some of those elements listed in the Hidden self work out, shown opposite.

When you try to establish a presence, what happens? For example, do you find yourself trying to be like a movie star with exaggerated gestures or self-important types of behaviour?

Hidden self work out

1 Find a quiet place where you will not be disturbed. Put a notepad and pen beside you.

2 Using the list of headings below to stimulate your thinking, see if you can produce one or more examples about yourself and your life.

- Irrational or absurd fears
- Strong dislikes or hatreds
- Loves and passions
- Unmet needs
- Hidden or unused talents
- Seldom expressed thoughts and feelings
- Past behaviour you are proud of that you rarely or never talk about
- Behaviour you feel bad about and seldom, if ever, think about
- Revealing stories or incidents
- Seldom expressed desires and wishes.

3 What does your list suggest about you? Is there anything on it that might be directly influencing how you behave when with other people, either positively or negatively?

Listen and trust your intuition

The Arctic Tern is a bird that lives seven degrees south of the North Pole and once a year flies 23,000 incredible miles back to its starting point. With a homing instinct like that it needs no fancy SatNav. Its instinct tells it where to go and how to get there. Humans too have an inbuilt ability to find our way through life and to home in on what is happening around us. Think of it as a radar, not something you can fit on a spreadsheet.

According to doctor of psychology Professor Cappon, who writes and researches the subject, intuition is the 'jewel in the crown of intelligence'. Compared with conscious reasoning, he argues that intuition is 'the secret of success in most human endeavours'.

Despite its apparent importance, though, not much about intuition surfaces in books or articles on communication or its role in building presence. This mainly reflects the assumption that it involves soft data and is therefore unreliable. Yet there is nothing irrational about intuition, even when it happens to be wrong. Some believe that we base 90 per cent of the decisions we make on intuition.

One accepted view of intuition is that at some hidden level you already know the answer and instinct merely lets you access it. For example, knowing someone is lying may not come directly from hearing their words, but from subtle physiological changes they cannot control but which give the game away. You may not even know you are recording these signs, yet unconsciously you are. By trusting your instinct, you allow this knowledge to surface.

While negotiating to buy the Atkins Computer Group in the UK, Jack Roseman, founder of two successful computer firms and president of a third, said: 'I can't tell you precisely what it was that told me within seconds that our only hope of acquiring the company was to win the hearts and minds of the managers sitting around the table.'

Asked by the owner whether he would like to see the accounts, Roseman used his intuition to respond that he wanted everyone to get to know each other first. If the chemistry was wrong, 'you could give me this company for nothing and I wouldn't want it'. This was exactly what people wanted to hear, and he won the deal, despite offering less money than his competitor.

There are many ways you might apply intuition when building your presence. Even when you have few hard facts to go on you might use:

- foresight – anticipating an event
- hindsight – understanding what caused something to happen
- hunch – the initial and likely answer to a problem
- knowing – being sure you know the best ways to reach a solution or use a discovery, or the best time to intervene or understand the significance of something.

You can sharpen and hone your intuition through practice and experimentation (see the following work outs).

Intuition work out

1 Set aside some specific times when you intend to explore your intuition – these could be when you are alone or, better still, when you are in a situation where you want to make a personal impact.
2 Use real issues and problems, not theoretical ones, to explore intuition. It works best in live situations rather than on meaningless tasks.
3 Allow yourself to examine what you are feeling and try to note how it is affecting you at that moment. For example, 'I feel tired right now and notice I'm getting increasingly impatient.'
4 Acknowledge or accept these feelings, even when uncomfortable. For example, 'I accept I'm angry right now and it's understandable I'm impatient.'
5 Treat your intuition as a quiet, respectful friend who usually waits to be asked for an opinion. Invite your intuition to give you a response. For example, 'I accept I am angry right now. What does this mean I should do next?'
6 Check your intuition's accuracy and your response to it.

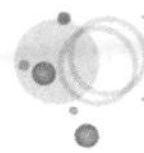

Additional intuition work out

1 **Diary**: Keep an intuition diary where you record impressions, whether they stem from dreams, sensations or instant thoughts. Examine these to see what insights they offer about your intuition – for example, when it seems to work best or in what environment.

2 **Interests**: Use your hobbies or interests to explore your intuition. Musicians have intuitions about music, scientists about science, parents about children, professionals about their particular subject.

3 **Answers**: Pick a problem or issue to which you want answers. Take a walk in green spaces and while enjoying your surroundings pick up an object such as a stone, a leaf or whatever is lying there. Look closely at it and ask your natural intuition: 'What insights can this give me about my question?'

Hints

- Treat with suspicion intuition that seems to be commanding you to do something, rather than suggesting possibilities.
- Combine your intuition with your logic.
- If you have an intuition, treat this with respect, as if it is advice given by a trusted colleague.

Preparing the body

As part of your preparation work to communicate your message, you may need to wake up your whole being, especially if you are giving a stand-up, formal presentation.

> tension before a live performance is perfectly natural

Tension before a live performance is perfectly natural; it is a form of concentrated energy to be properly harnessed. For example, before an important performance, actors spend an hour or more preparing their bodies. They work hard to unwind, relax and get themselves ready to communicate. Whenever you intend to achieve a strong Charisma Effect, you can usefully do this kind of preparation too. Using physical work you start taking control of the impact you want to make.

Particularly if you are giving a formal presentation, your body preparation work needs to be thorough and may consist of the following:

- Physical relaxation exercises: shake separate parts of your body to remove tension; close your eyes and focus on each part of the body in turn checking for tension; breathe deeply in and out slowly, while telling that part to let go and relax.
- Voice exercises to loosen up the throat and vocal cords: hum gently, make simple sounds such as aahhs and oos; say out loud a tongue twister, such as 'Red Leather, Yellow Leather, Red Leather, Yellow Leather', to help loosen your speech muscles.
- Stay away from smokers and avoid shouting or lengthy talking.

Physical warm-ups wake up your mind, body, breath and voice; they help make you fully ready to achieve your aim.

> *'Just being present emotionally in the scene, truly present emotionally, should be enough to convey what should be conveyed.'*
>
> Lasse Hallström, Swedish film director

Chapter 6
Authenticity

The legendary conductor, composer and pianist Leonard Bernstein was once asked by a photographer to pose for a picture inside an airport while sitting on a motorcycle. 'I don't ride a motorcycle,' Bernstein protested, 'it would be phony.' 'I'm sure you could ride it if you tried', the photographer replied.

To the amazement of his colleagues Bernstein jumped aboard, shot off at top speed across the airfield, slowed briefly to demonstrate a few tricky manoeuvres and returned to the shoot. 'Now,' he proclaimed, 'you can take your picture.'

We live in a world seemingly accelerating in the opposite direction to being authentic. Globalisation, lifestyle technology, spin doctors, advertising, virtual goods and services, online communities, even electronic lovers. They all conspire to undermine what is real or lasting, including human relationships.

A formula for how to be authentic would not be real. When someone is authentic they simply come across as themselves and not anyone else – there is no rule for how they do it. Quite simply, what you see is what you get. Everyone is born authentic. You don't see babies trying to be anyone but themselves. Starting in childhood and moving through adolescence and into adulthood, though, our spontaneity is knocked out of us, until we end up asking 'Who am I, really?'

a formula for how to be authentic would not be real

This separation becomes second nature. As adults, we may be reluctant or unable to remove the mask so people can see who we really are, directly affecting the impression we make on them. For example, Lord Reith, the first BBC chairman, was a hard-to-know person who had severe mood swings. At his daughter's wedding reception, her psychiatrist husband was told by a guest, 'I'd really like to meet Lord Reith.' To which the husband replied, 'So would I.'

As writer Marianne Williamson put it memorably: 'Our deepest fear is that we are powerful beyond measure. It is our light, not our darkness, that most frightens us. We ask ourselves, who am I to be brilliant, gorgeous, talented, fabulous? Actually, who are you not to be?' (This famous quote is often wrongly attributed to Nelson Mandela.)

Authenticity underpins strong charisma and proves particularly important if you happen to manage or lead people. But you cannot declare yourself to be authentic, it is up to other people to decide that you are.

Others first need to see you are true to yourself, know who you are and use that to communicate what you want. Former HR director of Marks & Spencer, Jean Tomlin, reportedly explained: 'I want to be me, but I am channelling parts of me to context. What you get is a segment of me. It is not a fabrication or a fake – just the bits that are relevant for that situation.'

Authenticity works through people identifying with you at a personal, human level. Putting it slightly differently, they feel connected in some way with who you are and what you stand for. To be authentic, people must hear your distinctive voice and experience those qualities that are unique to you.

Authentic performance on a personal level is the ability to express who you are, while being fully aware of the influence you are having around you. It is an act of dual attention. First you need self-awareness and, secondly, a sensitivity to the effect on your audience. This contributes to the chemistry we discuss later. It leads to an impactful first impression, a lasting impression and a sustainable relationship.

Being authentic produces benefits far beyond simply improving communications, teambuilding or promoting the brand. By removing the mask, people and indeed entire companies can become who they really are, knowing their purpose and their values. 'I couldn't be out of character, I just had to be myself', commented the larger than life Karen Darby on not being selected as one of the dragon judges on the TV series *Dragon's Den*, which aims to find budding entrepreneurs.

When you meet someone who is not being authentic or true to themselves you soon sense something is wrong. Sometimes we say 'he was putting on an act' or 'she is not entirely reliable'. Try the Authenticity work out to stimulate your thinking about what makes you authentic.

Authenticity work out

1 Think of three or four people you have met, read about or heard of who you admire a great deal. They might be alive or dead, from your own time or some time in history.

2 Narrow the names down to just one.

3 Write the person's name in the space below and then list what you most admire about them.

I really admire ....

What I most admire about this person is
(be as specific as possible)

....

....

....

....

....

....

4 Why does this person seem to be authentic?

5 How does this person convey authenticity in your view?

6 How do you convey authenticity?

Being authentic

If you really admire someone, it is perfectly understandable to want to be like them. But that is different from slavishly copying them in every way. You cannot be them – they are who they are and you are who you are. Being inauthentic is thinking or behaving as if you are someone you are not.

The obsession with celebrity encourages a lack of authenticity, leading us to believe we should aspire to instant fame or fortune without needing to be true to ourselves. For example, during the 1980s at the giant GE company, 'Everyone wanted to be like Jack Welch', explained Kevin Sharer, his long-term assistant and later also a CEO. Sharer learned at first hand that 'you need to be who you are, not try to emulate someone else'.

the obsession with celebrity encourages a lack of authenticity

During our Personal Impact learning events, we hear people say things like:

- 'I feel like I'm one person at work and another at home ... and I'm no longer sure which is me.'
- 'I'm tired of trying to figure out the hidden agendas; I wonder what we could accomplish if we all just got real?'

- 'I'm very adaptable, but I'm not sure that copying my boss's leadership style is the way to go.'
- 'I really want to be me, but it just wouldn't work in that place.'

So people come to work wearing their masks and wonder why they do not have the impact they want. Those attending the workshop often express amazement that what works about them comes from within, not from outside. Slightly incredulous they ask: 'You mean I just have to be myself?' When assured that is exactly what they need to be, you can feel the sense of relief.

People who try to use authenticity to convey charisma sometimes feel that this entitles them to let themselves go, showing anger, impatience or dissatisfaction, regardless of what it does to others. In fact, a reputation for authenticity needs to be carefully managed.

Am I being authentic?

'I don't believe a word you say,' said a journalist to a famous UK politician. 'Everything about you is phoney. Even your hair which looks like a wig isn't!' How do you know when you are not being entirely authentic? There are both internal and external warning signs.

The internal signs show that you feel somehow removed from what you are saying, disconnected from what really matters to you. You know you are 'putting on a front' and that the real you is not being allowed to emerge. You hide your thoughts, try to conceal your feelings and strongly censure what you actually say.

The external signs are that you start basing your actions not on what is right, but what is convenient or easy to go along with. You are open to pressure from others to do things that, when you think about it, you know are wrong or highly questionable.

'When Cameron threw "phoney" at him in Prime Minister's Questions, it stuck like napalm', argued one commentator about the impact of these words from the Conservative opposition leader on British prime minister Gordon Brown. Despite the apparent reduction in the importance of authenticity in favour of celebrity, still one of the most damaging accusations you can make about someone is to say they are phoney.

You cannot wake up one morning and simply declare, 'Today I am going to be authentic', because being authentic is not a goal, it is a process. You constantly adapt and recognise your fallibility. It is about:

- Your desire and ability to be real, not phoney or contrived. 'If you seek authenticity for authenticity's sake, you are no longer authentic', argued philosopher Jean-Paul Sartre – that is, we need to seek authenticity because it really matters to us in some way.
- How you connect with people, becoming worthy of their trust.

Warning signs you are not being authentic

- You make friends only with those who have something you want and might benefit you in the future.
- You are terrific at collecting business cards and phone numbers that will help you professionally, but have few real quality friendships or relationships.
- You manipulate others to get what you want without worrying about the effect this may have on them or yourself.
- You allow others to manipulate you.
- You focus your behaviour around gaining other people's approval, regardless of how you feel about them.
- You are not true to yourself.
- You feel lonely, disrespected and non-committal in your relationships.

- At work, you feel out of place, bored, underrated, unappreciated.
- You make little progress in your personal growth or do not even care about it.
- In your leisure time, you no longer enjoy *being* yourself, or you feel uncomfortable with those you once called your friends.
- You do not fully respect yourself and do not really believe in your own personal values or follow them in terms of actions.
- Even your compliments make people feel bad. They sound genuine at first but as the truth soaks in your real intention becomes clear.

We often sum up an authentic person and their personal impact on us as: 'What you see is what you get.' Almost absurdly, the easiest way to be more authentic is ... be more like yourself!

the easiest way to be more authentic is ... be more like yourself!

The comic George Burns once said of honesty, 'If you can fake it, you've got it made.' He could equally have been talking about authenticity. Faking authenticity, though, is much harder work than merely being yourself.

A study of over 1,000 business leaders, chosen for their authenticity and effectiveness, found they were constantly testing themselves through real-life experiences. They wanted to discover the purpose of their leadership and had learned that being authentic made them more effective. Even if you are not a leader in an organisation, this research finding is encouraging. It shows that being authentic is about a manageable process of constantly checking with reality, using it to determine 'Who am I?', 'What matters to me?', 'What do I want?' rather than expecting authenticity to instantly occur after intensive training or being born with an 'authentic' gene.

Style check

Your personal style affects how people experience your authenticity. For example, you may see your style as man or woman about town, cool and in control, but is that how you actually come across?

Imagine you had your own private public relations company working on your behalf or that a high-powered advertising agency was contracted to promote you to the world. One of the issues both sorts of experts would want to explore with you is:

- what is your personal brand?

Your brand contains everything you say and do; how you look, talk, think, move and behave. It's almost as if you were a company called, say, Me plc. What would be the Me plc brand? Just as we recognise that John Lewis, Zara, Apple or Nokia have their own styles and branding, so too does Me plc. The more you become aware of this brand, the more you will succeed at showing your authenticity and strengthen your Charisma Effect.

How would you describe each of these individuals' personal brands?

- Camilla
- Russia's Mr Putin
- Oprah Winfrey
- José Mourinho
- Gordon Ramsay
- Denzel Washington
- Andrew Marr.

Do they have a distinctive style, and if so what makes it so? How authentic does this tend to make them in your view?

Style work out (1)

Here are some ways to start reviewing and thinking about your personal style.

Complete the descriptions below and try to explain why you have chosen your various responses.

1 If I was a car, I would be a (e.g. a Mercedes) ....

because (e.g. I'm about quality and style) ....

....

2 If I was a food, I would be a (e.g. a grapefruit) ....

because (e.g. I am a bit sharp but good for you) ....

....

3 If I was a shop, I would be like (e.g. Marks & Spencer) ....

because (e.g. I give good value for what I have on offer) ....

....

- Looking at your answers, what do they suggest about your personal style?
- Would your friends or colleagues agree with your descriptions?
- How closely do you think you live the brand?
- Use the above to complete the second Style work out below.

....

....

Style work out (2)

At a meeting with your personal PR company or advertising agents, these experts want to convey your authenticity to the world. First, they decide to get a better picture of your personal brand, your particular style.

How would you describe your brand to them?

For example:

My brand is more like a Toyota than a BMW. I deliver quality without making a big fuss about it and don't push my style at you. I like to be seen as a brand that delivers to the customer – that is, I get things done and you can rely on me. I am also rather like some of the better stores, in that I don't get defensive if you find something wrong with what I do, I'll simply accept I got things wrong and try to put them right. I am also a bit like First Direct bank: I am easily accessible and when you do contact me I bet you find me friendly and patient.

....

....

....

....

....

....

....

....

Next, the consultants decide to design a logo that conveys who you are and what you stand for. What would this logo look like? Draw it, don't just describe it! Even if you cannot draw, try it all the same.

Reviewing the above, and also the results from the earlier Style work out, what have you learned about your style and how you come across?

Being yourself – your values

Any large gap between how you see yourself and how others experience you can potentially reduce your ability to convey authenticity and highlight what you need to work on. So let's look more closely at this aspect of being yourself. You are being authentic when you do the following.

- **Mean what you say and say what you mean**: Being consistent in your communication with people can strengthen your impact because people come to believe what you say. For example, when you make a promise, offer a compliment, make a threat, ask for help, do you really mean it? Any serious disconnection between your words and what you really mean damages your impact:
  - 'He's all hot air.'
  - 'Her bark is worse than her bite.'
  - 'He'll promise you the earth if … .'
  - 'With her it's always promises, promises.'
  - 'Do you really mean that?'
  - 'Thanks, but I wish I could be sure of that.'
  - 'I bet it'll never happen like that.'

  The better you are with words and talking the more important it is to match the words to your meaning. For example, when you are angry, happy, frustrated, busy, bored, confused, do you hide how you feel with bland phrases, platitudes and other distractions?

- **Convey you have clear principles and act on them**: What are your personal values? Do you know what you stand for and are you willing to share this with other people? Equally important, do people see you acting on what truly matters to you?

Many managers, for example, talk enthusiastically about customer care while their disillusioned staff witness them creating systems or processes that demonstrate quite the opposite. Be willing to use phrases like:

- 'What really matters to me is ... .'
- 'Here is where I stand on this ... .'
- 'I feel it is very important that ... .'
- 'I cannot go along with that because ... .'
- 'That would go against what I believe in, which is ... .'
- 'This is wrong because ... .'
- 'This is the right thing to do and I want to do it.'

- **Show you are reliable and can be depended upon**: Sure ways to signal 'you cannot depend on me' include turning up late for meetings, losing track of what people have asked you to do, agreeing to do things and then failing to deliver.

  When one of my close business colleagues agrees to send me a book or some information I need, he always writes it down meticulously on his action list, carried in a folder. Once it is down on that list I know for sure it will happen without fail. In 20 years of working with him I have seldom been let down.

  Being reliable and dependable is like gold plating your personal impact. Clearly one can still make a big impact even though unreliable, but this is despite such negative behaviour and not because of it.

- **Take responsibility for developing yourself to your full potential.**
- **Match your inner reality to its outward appearance.**

Values work out (1)

Round 1

Write a short mission statement that explains to you the following:

1 Why you think you are on this planet.

2 What really and truly matters to you – your values.

3 What you want to do to make your life meaningful.

Round 2

1 Revise this material until you are satisfied that it expresses what your life is all about.

2 Type it out.

3 Show it to someone you like and trust and ask them to share their reaction to it with you.

Round 3

1 In the light of the comments or response you have received, revise the material again until you feel satisfied with it.

2 Print out the material in large size (16 pt or bigger).

3 Put this material on your wall or where you will see it daily.

4 Read it every day and keep asking: 'Am I living the mission I want in my life?'

Values work out (2)

1 For the next seven days, keep track of any situations where other people try to get you to do things that contradict your personal values.

2 Write down the situations and how they made you feel.

3 How did you assert your right to act authentically?

Finally it is worth devising your own guidelines for practising the craft of authentic performance. For example, you might set yourself the following principles.

- Stay awake and be present.
- Notice your own bullshit.
- Allow yourself to be challenged on any inauthentic actions.
- Seek constant and honest feedback.
- Take a personal inventory of your values.
- Express yourself.
- Talk about what's important to you, rather than chit-chat.
- Be purposeful.
- Stay in touch with what you are passionate about.

> *'To be nobody but yourself, in a world which is doing its best, night and day, to make you everybody else, means to fight the hardest battle which any human being can fight; and never stop fighting.'*
>
> e e cummings, US poet

Chapter 7

Courage

There was an expectant buzz from the delegates. Shortly they would hear from an expert on inspirational leadership. Finally, the speaker entered from the back of the room and to people's amazement began singing. Striding towards the conference platform still singing loudly, people responded to his lyrics and their passionate, relevant message. Once he began speaking he had already captured their attention entirely, establishing an impressive Charisma Effect.

Are you willing to take risks to build your charisma? Or do you hate taking risks, while still wanting to improve your personal impact? If so, maybe it is time to do some self-awareness work around risk taking.

Although using interesting or challenging ways to communicate your message can definitely strengthen your charisma, being reckless could undermine it. For example, when meeting a new client you might risk making your point by reading a poem, showing a cartoon or even doing a magic trick. But, of course, to make the point by plunging a six-inch kitchen knife into the conference table would almost certainly appear reckless and do little to enhance your positive impact.

> courage is also not necessarily about dramatic risk taking

Courage is also not necessarily about dramatic risk taking – it can be as simple as daring to use your physicality more actively to get yourself across to people. If you are naturally expressive with your hands, face and body then courage may not be an issue, but for many people deliberately being more expressive using their physical being can certainly seem to demand courage.

To develop courage in your interpersonal communications you need both regular practice and plenty of feedback. If necessary, make sure you ask for it.

Intelligent risk taking

It is worth taking risks that help get your message across when you have weighed up whether:

- the benefits would outweigh the costs if it all goes wrong
- there is only a remote chance of the worst case situation actually happening (see the upside–downside box, opposite).

Also, what appears to be risky or to demand a great deal of courage may on closer examination prove just to be a fear of shadows. Working with your fear is therefore part of developing your courage to be different. Try the Fear work out below.

Fear work out

- Find a quiet, safe place where you will not be disturbed for at least half an hour.
- Lie on the floor, feet up on a chair, with a thin cushion under your head.
- Take long, slow breaths, keeping it deep and steady.
- Start to speak your fears aloud, 'I am frightened of …'.
- Begin with objects or animals, such as spiders, cars, computers.
- Now move on to events, such as giving a talk, entering a room full of strangers, meeting the boss privately.

- Next mention the people you feel frightened of: a parent, boss, a partner, a sibling, a colleague at work.
- Finally, say aloud the names of people or events from your past that generated fear. Do they still exist? What do you currently fear most right now – flooding, terrorism, loss of health? What do you fear in the future?
- Make sure you say the fears out loud, not safely inside your head.

During this work out you may feel tearful, anxious or find your body is tensing up and you have an urge to get up and do something entirely different. Stick with it though, since by naming your fears they begin to lose their power over you.

Upside–downside: making sense of risk taking

1 You ask a client for the order you have been diligently chasing.
   - Worst case downside = client refuses; decides to end the relationship.
   - Best case upside = you get the order; establish a long-lasting, profitable relationship.
2 In a one-to-one session, you demand that a colleague improves her performance.
   - Worst case downside = the person gets angry; resigns claiming you are bullying or showing unfair discrimination.
   - Best case upside = person thanks you for your frankness; agrees to try harder and afterwards sings your praises to others.
3 You enter a room and talk to the first person you see who is free to engage with you.
   - Worst case downside = person rejects your approach rudely; walks away leaving you feeling awful.
   - Best case upside = person responds with enthusiasm; you make a friend or business contact for life; it leads to a major contract.

In each case, what is the chance of the worst case actually happening? If it is extremely small, then the risk may be worth taking, given the potential best case situation or some variation on it happening.

Making these kinds of mental calculations is what intelligent risk taking is about.

You need emotional resilience to handle possible unfavourable results from your risk taking. Such resilience usually only comes through experimenting and exploring the risky area.

Strangely, some people feel fine about taking physical risks, such as climbing, abseiling or whitewater rafting, while strenuously avoiding the social risks needed to get their message across with impact.

Whether you are an introvert or an extrovert may also influence your risk taking. For example, extroverts may find risk taking fun, seeing it as just part of being sociable and assertive. By contrast, introverts may find it distasteful. While you cannot easily move from being one to the other, it can help to become more aware of how your basic personality may be inhibiting or encouraging risk taking.

extroverts may find risk taking fun

Risk taking that builds your charisma may mean you:

- show the courage to challenge or question people
- have a point of view and express it
- stand up for your beliefs in the face of opposition
- accept alternative views without being defensive
- make full use of physical expression.

Let's look at these more closely.

Challenge or question people

A new CEO of an insurance company called a town hall meeting to introduce himself to all the staff. After the formal introductions, he took the risk of telling a personal story about dealing with a travel agency. He shared with everyone how the agency's outstanding customer care made him feel, how he experienced a burst of gratitude to the agency for resolving what could have been a frustrating and worrying problem. Looking around the packed room, the new CEO asked if anyone else had recently experienced exceptional customer care.

Soon people who would never normally have spoken to a chief executive in public began sharing their own stories of customer care. At just the right moment, the CEO smiled and explained his vision that people who dealt with his new company would talk to their friends in just this way about its wonderful customer care.

There was an awkward silence and at last someone ventured: 'But we always have good ratings in the annual industry measures for customer care.' The CEO nodded, 'I absolutely agree, so it's clear we have a strong platform on which to build something truly outstanding. That is what I want to do, it's an absolute commitment of mine and I want it to be yours too.'

After the meeting, people often talked at length about the new CEO and how he had come across and excited them with his vision of the future. No one mentioned charisma, but the CEO had conveyed it strongly through his challenge and questioning.

Do you feel comfortable challenging people and confronting them over things which you disagree about? People with strong personal impact usually have the courage to question the status quo, deal with conflict and ask awkward questions, even when they may alienate some people.

While challenge can be charisma enhancing, it normally needs to be constructive, rather than destructive. If you constantly complain about situations, always raise impossible-to-answer questions, seldom agree with people about anything or generally prove hard to work with, people will see you as offering an unwelcome kind of challenge.

Constructive challenge, on the other hand, stimulates because it can inject fresh thinking, offer alternatives to consider and engage people's interest. Nor is it always necessary to feel comfortable doing it; those on the receiving end merely need to see you are challenging in a spirit of enquiry, rather than, say, vindictiveness.

People with a strong charisma perfect ways of posing the right questions so they enliven, rather than threaten. Part of this may stem from offering challenge in a friendly manner; it may also come from not making people wrong.

An example

Destructive challenge:	'Your strategy makes no sense to me, how on earth did you arrive at it?'
Constructive challenge:	'Could you take me through your strategy so I can understand how you arrived at it?
Destructive challenge:	'Our customer care is rubbish and you know it.'
Constructive challenge:	'Our current customer care seems to have plenty of scope for improvement; do you agree?'
Destructive challenge:	'Why did you mess up delivering this report on time again?'
Constructive challenge:	'What do you think is preventing you getting your reports in on time? '

Challenge work out

Change the following challenges from destructive into constructive ones.

'You couldn't be more wrong. We just don't do it that way.'

....

'It's happening again. This team is wasting time on yet another pointless debate.'

....

'If you can find a better supplier than us let me know.'

....

'This agenda is nonsense, why don't we focus on the really important issues?'

....

'Well, it may inspire you, but it doesn't inspire me.'

....

Now create three real constructive challenges for others in your life.

....

....

....

Have a point of view and express it

If you do not know where you are going, any road will do. Without a point of view you become less interesting to others and weaken your charisma. People making a strong personal impact usually have something to say for themselves, using phrases like:

- 'My view is …'
- 'The way I see it is …'
- 'I can't agree with that because …'
- 'What matters to me about this is …'
- 'What I want is …'
- 'I would prefer that …'
- 'From my point of view …'

Do you sometimes find it hard to know what your opinion actually is about an issue or situation? So you sit silent in meetings, finding it difficult to take a clear position on the subject under discussion. There may be several reasons why this happens.

First, the issue or situation seems outside your knowledge or experience. Second, you may actually possess a point of view yet cannot readily access it at that moment. This leads to those frustrating times when later you realise what you could have said, but did not. A third reason arises when you have a cultural background where you are not normally expected to express an opinion, especially without being asked for it.

if you do not know where you are going, any road will do

Whatever the reason, you can start generating your own point of view about an issue by preparing, asking questions and gaining more information, relating it to something familiar.

Preparation can often provide you with a whole range of opinions, which in the heat of the moment can otherwise seem out of reach. Try to attend a meeting, a one-to-one session or other important communication situation with something ready to say. There will often be plenty of sources to stimulate you, such as a pre-planned agenda, the topic itself, reading widely, talking to other people in advance and so on.

Asking questions will often open up a topic, stimulating you to come up with an opinion, using additional information. Ask open-ended questions to encourage people to provide more than a simple yes or no answer.

Relating the issue to something familiar can be a creative stimulus to arriving at an opinion. For example, you could use:

- your personal values
- past experience or something it reminds you of
- an existing policy or guideline
- others' strong opinions and how these make you feel
- something entirely unconnected to generate a fresh insight.

Express it

Having an opinion is not enough, you also need the courage to express it. Sometimes this means offering your opinion without being asked. At other times it may be better to wait until a suitable moment arises when people will be ready to receive it.

Once people realise you often have an opinion they will start looking forward to hearing it. Incidentally this is why you see people starting to look towards certain individuals expectantly during meetings. They know from experience that these people have views and anticipate hearing them.

Staying silent and withholding your opinion may create a useful air of mystery, but if you force people to work hard to extract your views this just limits your impact. Instead, generate your point of view, listen for a break in the flow of conversation, be brave and express it.

If everyone seems too busy talking, this could mean it is best to stay quiet. However, you could be leaving the field open to those who make the most noise, and thus never get your opinion across.

If there is no break in the conversation, try the quiet voice in the background technique. You wait until someone winds down a bit and say clearly without aggression, 'I would like to say something please.' If people ignore you, repeat it again, even if you have to talk over someone else. Go on saying, 'I would like to say something please', increasingly loudly, until at last people have to stop and listen. It takes a certain amount of courage to use this technique but it will guarantee you an attentive audience.

Watch out for the opinion trap, where you find yourself becoming dogmatic, over-assertive and excessively pushing your views, regardless of whether other people want to hear them. A version of the opinion trap awaits unwary managers or leaders. Because people constantly seek your opinions you start assuming you must always immediately pronounce on what you think is right or wrong or what should be done. This instant offering of an opinion can undermine your personal impact, unless you are being complimentary – for example, noticing something done well or congratulating someone on an achievement.

watch out for the opinion trap

The opinion trap also occurs when people start telling you their problems. Unwary sales people often fall into it, believing the client is actually asking for advice. In fact the person merely wants to share an issue, without being offered an immediate fix.

Develop your ability to listen with your whole attention by offering clarifying questions such as:

- 'Do other people feel the same?'
- 'How does this make you feel?
- 'Is this something fairly recent?'
- 'Sounds awful, what does your boss think?'
- 'Have you ever had this happen before?'
- 'What do you think they want in return?'

- 'Do you look forward to that?'
- 'Can you explain that a bit more?'

Stand up for your beliefs

'My real test of courage,' says Jacqueline Gold, chief executive of the highly successful Ann Summers retail chain that sells sexy lingerie and adult toys, 'is to be in the minority on many occasions.'

Gold's Charisma Effect consists of great poise combined with her courage to stand her ground and speak her mind about what really matters to her. She is nowhere near the far end of the Charisma Spectrum, yet her impact remains powerful and memorable.

'You don't like my principles? I have plenty of others', joked Groucho Marx and, in reality, many people seem like that. Faced with criticism, rejection or hostility they simply crumble. Rather than risk any conflict, instead they lapse into resentful silence or, worse, disown what they have previously put forward.

Achieving a strong personal impact partly stems therefore from being willing to stand up for your views, taking the risk of facing down opposition. Unless you are also spoiling for a fight, this need not involve a heated argument. Instead, you simply assert your right to hold your view or to hold certain values and demand that others treat this with respect.

A useful way to stand up for your beliefs is to respond by showing respect for the opposition, rather than decrying it. You say things like:

- 'I hear what you say, yet I see it rather differently.'
- 'I realise you disagree, and I'd also like my views to be taken seriously.'
- 'You obviously feel strongly about this and so do I.'
- 'That is one interpretation. I have a different one.'
- 'What really matters to me is … .'

It can feel risky standing up for your point of view, especially if no one else seems to immediately support you, but this isolation may be misleading. Once people see you standing up for your views you may begin to attract supporters.

Accept alternative views

There is something engaging about a person with a clear point of view who does not seem to push it at you, as if trying to instantly convert you to their position. Strengthen your personal impact by showing you have the courage to hear alternative views, without becoming defensive.

As outlined in Chapter 3 on fluency, try using the technique of accept and build: when a person puts forward a different view from yours, rather than disparage it you try to build on it. You may even be able to link it to your own views and strengthen your own position further.

Use physical expression

Most of us do not realise the significance of bodily cues or even associate them with courage. Yet physical expression can take courage and when you see people making a strong personal impact they seldom appear afraid to make definite and sometimes expansive gestures. This may include using their body in positive ways to convey their message, whether remaining extremely still, laughing uproariously, intense listening, or using their hands to emphasise their point.

most of us do not realise the significance of bodily cues

Do you walk around as if you are a success or a failure? How do you look when you enter a room? Do people get an immediate impression of self-confidence or of self-doubt? Using your charisma means having the courage to reject, at least temporarily, any sense of low self-esteem in favour of an assertive, self-assured presence.

Actors learn early in their training that how they hold themselves mentally on stage rapidly translates into how they appear physically. For example, they practise walking as if they were complete failures, then as if they owned the whole world. Courage in this sense could simply be to choose to hold yourself physically as having high status, rather than low status.

Try the Status work out below.

Status work out

1 Find an empty room with plenty of space to walk around.
2 From a pack of playing cards extract a set of ace to 10 in value.
3 Shuffle these cards and pick one at random.
4 This number defines your status from 1 = low to 10 = very high.
5 Using this number, start walking around the room as if this is now your status in life.
6 Pick a second number and again walk around feeling what it would be like to have that status in life. Enter a room with that 'persona'.
7 Finally, do it yet again and experiment with this third level of status.
   - What have you learned from doing this?
   - How did your body behave at the various different status levels?
   - How did you feel in each case?
   - What did this work out tell you about how you might enter a room next time?

Actor David Tennant was forced to bow out of the sold-out London run of *Hamlet* before the official first night in 2009. He was suffering from a chronic back injury that required surgery and the critics assumed he would permanently make way for his talented understudy.

Courage, though, often underpins a person's charisma. A leading critic hailed Tennant's triumphant return performance as 'led by an actor of extraordinary courage and charisma who has made a persuasive claim to true greatness.'

Charisma also implies boldness, the courage to stand apart from other people. It could mean taking certain risks that others would not accept, ranging from being willing to touch someone physically while talking to them, to taking some unusual action that gains attention for your message.

Another way in which courage may surface with charisma is a willingness to lead from the front, set an example and show the way. Leaders of the most successful companies, for example, tend to be both humble and fearless.

Joan of Arc won the loyalty of battle-hardened veterans through her unusual vision, her steely determination and particularly her physical courage. When an arrow went through her shoulder during the battle for the city of Tourelles, she had it removed then returned to take part in the final assault.

More recently Boris Yeltsin's courage and charisma brought an end to the communist party and the Soviet Union itself. His enemies may never forgive him, but the sight of him standing heroically against the attempted coup of August 1991 remains unforgettable.

Perhaps most challenging of all, charisma courage allows people to see behind your mask to the real you. By showing your vulnerability, for instance, people come to see you as incredibly human. Often that alone is a source of magnetism and inspiration.

> *'Just being present emotionally in the scene, truly present emotionally, should be enough to convey what should be conveyed.'*
>
> Lasse Hallström, Swedish film director

Chapter 8

Passion

'The best leaders I know are passionate about what they do,' reported Alan Leighton, Chairman of the Royal Mail, after interviewing some of Britain's top business people. If the word 'passion' makes you queasy, then how do you feel about commitment or enthusiasm?

Research conducted by British Professor Richard Wiseman studied participants of FameLab, a national competition to find the new 'faces of science'. Those most able to transmit their emotions to others progressed furthest in the competition, using their personalities to impress a panel of judges.

Despite its known power to affect oneself and others, there is nothing spooky or beyond reach about passion. Often it is just a case of reconnecting with a long-forgotten part of oneself, which has been allowed to atrophy. At other times it is a case of allowing one's commitment to shine through.

there is nothing spooky or beyond reach about passion

Passion is not only useful when talking about your major life interest, it is also valuable for communicating about less exalted, day-to-day issues. For example, when discussing with a client your company's service, you will be more effective if you show a genuine commitment to that service and want to share it.

You will make more impact when you feel an issue is really important and convey this through using your natural enthusiasm. Passion has the ability to influence other people's emotions, thinking and even behaviour. So it is worth exploring your own self-awareness around this whole issue.

Not sure about your passion, what excites you or gets the adrenaline flowing? Try the various work outs below to look more closely at your life and the key events that made you the person you are.

Firm up your passion work out (1)

Looking at the past

1 Use the picture below to draw your lifeline. Create your own large version, if possible at least A3 size.

2 **For home and life in general**, including interests and hobbies, plot the highs and lows, events that caused you joy or sorrow, made you proud, excited, etc.

   Show the strong, transition points when things fundamentally changed you, making you the person you are today.

3 Which of these events made the most impression and why?

4 **For your career**, make a second chart and plot the highs and lows, the points where you felt most excited and where you were most bored or demotivated.

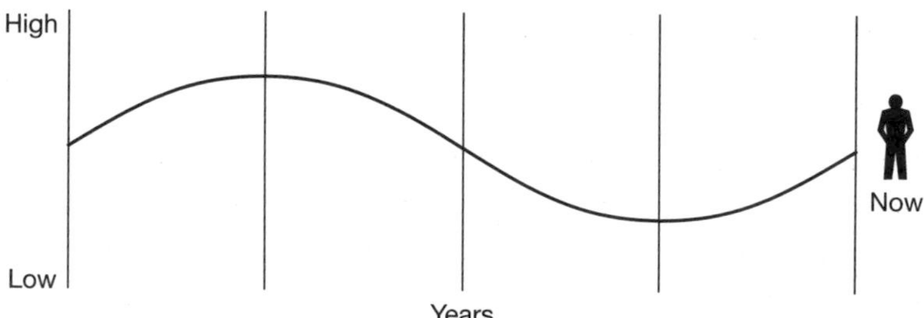

Timeline 1: How did I get there?

Firm up your passion work out (2)

Looking to the future

1 Use the same A3-size paper to *look ahead just one year*. List what you would most like to change in each of the areas you recorded on the previous chart.

2 *Now try looking ahead three years*. How would you reach these things and what steps would you need to take to reach these goals? Start dreaming about your aims. Don't worry if they seem fanciful or even impossible.

3 *Finally, look ahead a full five years from now*. What would your life look like then? What will have changed? What could you do to make it happen?

4 Use the timeline to write down your thoughts and feelings about the various issues you have recorded.

5 What are some of the underlying themes? What seems to be present no matter what the situation? What values seem to matter most in your timeline?

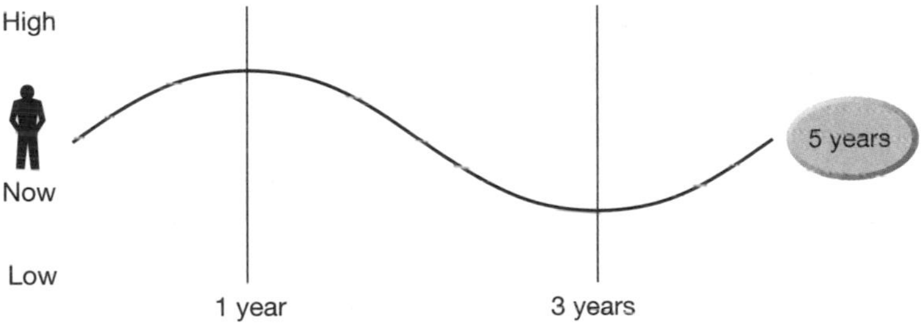

Timeline 2: Where do I want to be?

Genuine enthusiasm is nearly always infectious, and the more uninhibited you become the greater its likely impact on others. Obviously, you can overdo the 'look how excited I am' form of communication and consequently make some people feel uneasy. Yet, on balance, it is better to be over-enthusiastic and risk a negative response than to play it safe and keep your passion under lock and key.

It is a myth that people, especially the so-called reserved British, frown upon enthusiasm and therefore it should be avoided at all costs. This usually only occurs when people become so over-excited it seems they have lost any sense of reality.

Questions to ask yourself

- Am I excited about what I wish to communicate?
- What exactly excites me about this issue?
- Why should other people be excited by it too?

Confidence and passion

Do you ever wonder about the secret of those people who seem to exude confidence and self-belief? How do they do it? Is it upbringing, high status, wealth, education, career success or what? As explained in Chapter 4, confidence does not simply happen. It is a result of practice and through acquiring competence that ultimately confidence is generated.

When you fully connect with your passion or commitment, though, it can automatically start to build your confidence. This happens because in sharing your passion you are, in effect, practising speaking about what really matters to you. That in itself can build confidence.

Once you become entirely absorbed by the meaning of your message, you cannot easily contain yourself, which leaves little space for feeling nervous.

> **Questions to ask yourself**
>
> - How confident am I about what I want to communicate?
> - Why does the issue I want to communicate matter to me?
> - Why should it matter to others?
> - If I was totally confident, how would it affect what I say?

Spontaneity and passion

When you act openly, with spontaneity, you are likely to create an atmosphere that is equal and honest. If people see you speaking from the heart, not just from the head, it can be infectious, often prompting them to act that way too.

How comfortable are you thinking on your feet and accepting things as they come? Do you feel nervous, preferring to stick closely to whatever actual or mental script you have chosen?

how comfortable are you thinking on your feet?

Lack of practice provides one common reason for being fearful of thinking on one's feet. Unless you graduated in advanced physics, if someone asked you to talk without preparation to 500 people for 15 minutes on Einstein's Theory of Relativity you may well find it difficult. Yet it is seldom lack of knowledge that makes thinking on one's feet such a challenge.

Or perhaps you believe that thinking on your feet requires a lightning response, a razor-sharp brain producing instant insights? This may be true if you want to be a stand-up comedian improvising on the spot or someone engaged in clever repartee. Generally, thinking on your feet merely requires you to stay in touch with what you care about and therefore enables you to draw on your inner resources without restraint.

While spontaneity cannot by definition be entirely planned, you can fertilise the ground in which it flourishes, through anticipation, listening, questioning, big picture thinking and buying time.

- **Anticipation**: There are many situations in which you can predict you may need to act spontaneously, without having a formal route map to follow. For example, you may be asked to give an instant speech, talking off the cuff about something. Humorist Mark Twain boasted it always took him several weeks to prepare a good spontaneous speech, meaning that he was always ready in some way for these challenges.
- **Listening**: People will often provide you with important clues and information about what they are thinking and feeling. Through attentive listening and watching, you can usually pick these up so you become ready to respond when necessary.
- **Big picture thinking**: Whatever issue is under discussion, try and see it with fresh eyes; extend your thinking. For example, when searching for a response try asking yourself: 'What is this really about?', 'What might be missing here?', 'What does this remind me of?', 'How does this relate to my own experience?', 'What is this issue telling me about the situation I now face?'
- **Buying time**: Give yourself more room to be spontaneous through buying time before you respond.
  - Wait for a speaker to completely finish before attempting to give a response.
  - Offer a question of your own.
  - Ask for some thinking time.
  - Make noises such as 'hmmm' to show you are paying attention but are still thinking.
  - Use filler phrases like 'That's a good point', 'This could have lots of implications', 'We need to talk more about this.'

- Reflect back on something the speaker has said, 'So what you seem to be saying is ...'
- Without offering an immediate response, tell a story that reminds you about this issue, while continuing to think how best to respond.

Questions to ask yourself

- Am I willing to be spontaneous in getting across my communication?
- What might get in the way of my willingness to act spontaneously?
- How can I best prepare to make the most of certain likely situations?

Challenge and passion

When you encounter people with a passion or commitment they tend to question ways of doing things, have strong opinions on certain situations, press for action and in many cases show an uncomfortable readiness to rock the boat.

Driven by their passion such people seem courageous, yet in practice they are simply committed to their aim. In pursuit of it they are willing to confront, raise uncomfortable issues or question what is happening. Yet underneath these same people may be anxious or unsure of themselves.

How you challenge is as important as the challenge itself. If in doing so you make the other person wrong, feel disrespected or in some way attacked, this may undermine, rather than enhance your impact. Try challenging as if in search of information:

- 'Is that how everybody feels right now?'
- 'What can we do to change this situation do you think?
- 'This does not seem right to me, what are your views on this?'
- 'Where do we go from here?'

- 'This seems wrong to me – anyone else feel the same way?
- 'Would it be possible to do it differently next time?

The more you allow your passion free rein, the more you need to ensure your challenges spring from a positive source, rather than defensiveness, lack of confidence or a desire to make someone else look bad.

> **Questions to ask yourself**
>
> - Why do I need to challenge?
> - When did I last make a challenge using my passion?
> - What kind of challenges am I unwilling to make and why?
> - Who am I least willing to challenge and disagree with?
> - Do I challenge from a position of seeking information or do I tend to challenge so that people feel attacked?

Energy and passion

To communicate with passion and enthusiasm demands energy. It is energy you put into how you speak and behave. You cannot convey passion for your message while talking in a boring monotone, sitting slumped in your chair, not looking people in the eye or allowing your head to drop to your chest as if half asleep.

Energy used to convey passion takes many forms, including your physicality – how you move and act, your voice, smiling or, in some cases, your mastery of public speaking.

> energy used to convey passion takes many forms

When you exhibit a high level of energy it helps make you visible, establishing your presence. If you feel this is a relevant issue for you, then set out to become more aware of your energy levels at different times and notice that, when these seem low, this tends to reduce your ability to convey commitment.

Without energy even the most powerful message or most persuasive speaker will go unheard.

Questions to ask yourself

- When was the last time I really used energy to convey commitment or passion for some message?
- Do I regularly put energy into how I convey my essential messages?
- How is this energy mainly displayed – in gestures, voice, visual appearance?

Fun, playfulness and passion

Using passion does not mean you must always come across as deadly serious. It may be equally effective to have fun talking about your passion by creating a sense of playfulness around it. For example, you might use your natural humour to get across your strong message or refuse to take yourself too seriously and create a sense of enjoyment around conveying your core message to people.

Ways to generate a sense of fun and playfulness around your message are limited only by your imagination and your readiness to take risks. This might include singing your message, reading a poem, wearing a funny hat, dressing up, audience participation, telling a story against yourself, using interesting words, metaphors or stories, cartoons, movie clips, in fact just about anything that allows you and your audience to see the amusing side of things and receive your message.

Passion is the future

We have seen that to enhance your Charisma Effect a vital ingredient is being able to identify and fully use your passion. Reassuringly, the world is gradually moving in that direction too, with more and more awareness of its importance not just for the individual who needs to make an impact, but entire organisations.

As Gary Hamel, the widely respected commentator on business, puts it, the future of companies in the twenty-first century is to build an environment that 'cherishes human initiative, creativity and passion.' Using your passion is exactly what your colleagues may really need, and when you properly exploit it you will certainly make a powerful impression.

> *'One person with passion is better than forty people merely interested.'*
>
> E. M. Forster, novelist

Chapter 9

Demeanour

If you are a pop star or an eccentric millionaire you probably do not need to worry much about your general appearance and manner – your demeanour. But if you are neither, then it can seriously affect your personal impact.

Demeanour is a handy, if rather posh, word for your manner. This includes how you carry yourself, your grooming, general appearance and image. Each has an influence on how people experience you and each may need some attention as part of making sure you make the best of being yourself.

> demeanour is a handy, if rather posh, word for your manner

For example, in an eight-year battle over patent infringement the judges complained that an expert witness potentially lost all credibility 'due to shifty eyes and poor demeanour'. In his swan song budget in 2007, the then chancellor Gordon Brown, conscious of his reputation for being dour and controlling, put on a jaunty demeanour by cracking jokes and affecting a light-hearted manner.

A successful warehouse manager for a major UK electronics company really looked the part. Complete with shiny suit, slicked down hair and pointy shoes, he felt fine with his appearance, until he got an important new job working for the BBC, where he was expected to present to senior executives. His unchanged appearance now proved too alien to the culture of the organisation he had joined. His inappropriate demeanour undermined his ability to make an impact.

Being neat, clean and fresh may seem enough. Perhaps you are also someone who believes substance counts more than outward appearance? However, because people initially have little else to go on when making judgements about you, your general demeanour can be all-important.

How would you describe your outward appearance? Would people call you well-dressed, dapper, smart, stylish, conventional, or merely drab and ordinary? What is the image you want to convey, not just on those special occasions when you take particular trouble to look good? When you put out your clothes to wear, either on the day or in preparation for it, what is the impression you want to make? Who is the person you want people to encounter? Try the Appearance work out below.

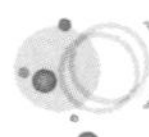

Appearance work out

Find a full-length mirror, as in a department store's changing rooms. (Consider installing one at home as part of improving your demeanour.)

Wearing your normal work clothes, look long and hard at what you see in the mirror. This is different from the earlier mirror work out in Chapter 2. In this work out, view yourself for care, flair and aware.

- **Care**: Does the person in the mirror seem to take care of themselves? What are the signs of care – for example, crumpled or fresh looking, shoes scruffy or smart? Hair a mess or orderly? What changes would you recommend to this person about their appearance?
- **Flair**: What makes you look distinctive? Does anything stand out or is everything bland in terms of look, colour or design? What changes would introduce some flair – for example, more or fewer colours, higher-quality clothing, more stylish look?
- **Aware**: How appropriate is your appearance to your working life? Does it fully align with the message you want to send people about your charisma and the impact you want to make?

Does your image suit the job? Take, for instance, a go-ahead young woman executive from the music industry who attended one of our Personal Impact courses. She held a responsible job in her company, having graduated from art school, yet in sartorial terms she had never really moved on. She continued dressing in excessively tight-fitting blouses that, while fine back at college, now made her look a flirt.

Using video and a mirror, and perhaps with a little external feedback, you can make a useful start to improving and strengthening your demeanour. As with your overall communication purpose discussed in Chapter 2, start thinking about the following:

- What image do I want to project?
- What image do I fear projecting?
- How big is the gap?
- How can I eliminate the gap and still be me?

Take, for example, Peter D, who started as an independent management consultant. With an already persuasive Charisma Effect, he began achieving meetings with senior company executives, yet he wore cheap suits from high-street chain stores. Meanwhile those he hoped to advise usually dressed in stylish, costly gear that enhanced their obvious status.

Eventually, an experienced fellow consultant kindly explained: 'If you are going to deal with senior people who wear immaculate, distinctive apparel, you cannot get away with looking cheap.' Peter immediately went out and ordered two top-of-the-range business suits. From then on he never looked back, confidently dealing with his growing list of prestigious clientele on equal terms.

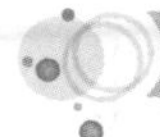

Awareness work out

1. At your next team or business meeting take a systematic look at how people are dressed and their overall appearance. Does it enhance or undermine their impact?
2. Contact three trusted friends or colleagues to ask for frank feedback on your grooming.
3. Ask them to describe how they see your general dress sense. Would they describe it as stylish, dapper, careless, casual, low key, etc.?
4. Next ask them to say how they see your general grooming, such as clean, neat, attention to detail, etc.
5. Next ask, 'Do I have any annoying habits or gestures that you think might get in the way of making a strong impression?'
6. Finally ask them how they see your physical appearance, such as overweight, thin, stooped, upright, good bearing, etc.
7. Obtain a video camera and film yourself entering a room and standing – what message do you seem to project, are your clothes appropriate, what works about your appearance?
8. Use all this information to make changes in your general grooming.

Demeanour may sound like jargon and be hard to nail down precisely, but it starts with first impressions. Based on them, people make assumptions about your:

- economic status – rich, poor, successful, average
- educational level – graduate, basic attainment, drop out
- trustworthiness – honest, believable, reliable
- social status – quality, high-flyer, mixes well, oddball, loner, moving up or moving down
- level of sophistication – cool, confident, anxious, at ease
- attitude – aggressive, friendly, easy-going, hard to know.

Such judgements can occur in seconds, which is why demeanour can be so critical. One study of recruitment, for example, found good grooming actually produced more favourable hiring decisions than actual job qualifications.

Let's put this whole issue of demeanour on a more business-like footing. What are you willing to invest in your appearance and manner? It may be a cliché to talk of personal branding – as if you were a bar of soap or a car – yet this remains a useful benchmark for assessing your willingness to invest in yourself and how you come across.

what are you willing to invest in your appearance and manner?

- How strong is your brand (your image)?
- What does it need in the way of a refresh or an upgrade?
- Does your brand speak quality?
- Can you afford not to invest in it?

When appearance does not fully match your desired brand image it is time to invest in change, but this does not mean altering your entire personality. To improve your personal impact means spending time and resources on developing various aspects of general demeanour. This could include your wardrobe, posture, grooming, handshake, manners, image and so on.

Your wardrobe

This is the most obvious area where you can make rapid changes. For example, if you are a man, do you stick to a drab palette of black, grey, blue and the occasional khaki-coloured neutral? If you are a woman, are you frightened of wearing clothes that could be construed as showy rather than functional?

High-powered women in particular will often firmly declare that, 'I am not interested in fashion', implying that senior women are supposed to be above it all, that fashion is for secretaries and lesser mortals. Dig deeper and they will often reveal a yearning for being able to dress fashionably.

While it may be unhealthy to let fashion rule your life, to ignore the power of clothes is nothing to be proud of either. In fact it could be a form of arrogance or a sign of being out of touch with reality.

There are seven common mistakes that people make about their clothing.

Mistake number 1: Cheap and cheerful

If you are determined to improve your impact quality, it is an investment, not extravagance, to buy quality, especially in the business world. Cheap is ultimately expensive; not only because it can harm your image, but in the simple cost per times worn.

Mistake number 2: Ignore fashion

Certain fashion looks date you, and you ignore these at your peril. It is no use saying, 'I am not interested in fashion', since it is not you who cares, it's your audience.

Fashion is confusing, transitory but rather less arbitrary than you might think. Today, all fashion alters so quickly that, paradoxically, one of the best solutions is to invest in a classic look that refuses to date. While more expensive in the short term, classic looks pay back handsomely in the longer term.

Mistake number 3: Poorly fitting clothes

If they fit badly, even the best clothes can be a disaster. A good fit is so essential it is worth paying the extra tailoring cost to get what you want.

If you want to look well turned out and noticeable, common mistakes like items being too tight, the wrong length or a strained fit are unacceptable.

Mistake number 4: Lack of co-ordination

Make sure your clothes blend in with each other correctly or the whole effect can be entirely ruined. Colour co-ordination can make or break a person's appearance, so give this area of your grooming some thought.

If you do not entirely trust your instincts to buy items that go together appropriately, consider investing in learning about the basic principles of colour co-ordination. There are some simple guidelines, such as how to ensure the colour in a major item of clothing also reflects minor accessories; when to put a light item with a dark item; when one colour does not go with another; or what colour best suits your particular complexion. These can all help improve your co-ordination.

Mistake number 5: The other bits don't matter

Accessories are the small details that make a statement. Badly chosen ties, hat, bag, belt, gloves, shoes, socks and even an umbrella can potentially damage your image and you may never know it.

Make sure accessories underpin not undermine your image. For example, items of jewellery can be dangerous territory for a man, especially someone wanting to climb the corporate ladder. A glittering earring may be acceptable on a famous footballer but will it help your impact too? For women, flashy belts, garish jewellery and face studs can be fine outside work, yet seriously reduce your personal impact in the work arena.

Mistake number 6: Small image killers

Like inappropriate accessories, small image killers leave a nasty taste and yet can easily be prevented, once you become aware of them. Here are some to avoid:

- fraying – collars, cuffs or signs of wear
- badly pressed clothes – do not impress

- spots – on ties, dresses or suits
- buttons missing, loose or undone
- jacket sleeves or trouser lengths too long or short
- shoes – scruffy, unpolished or in need of repair
- shabby belts.

Mistake number 7: Do not be distinctive

In the early history of computer giant IBM, just about every man – and it was only men in those days – wore the company uniform of blue suit, white shirt and carefully matching tie. The days of IBM clones have mainly gone but, with the exception of start-ups and high-tech firms, there remains a huge pressure on employees within many organisations to conform and avoid standing out from the crowd. Yet it is a mistake to assume your wardrobe must be entirely bland and impersonal.

it is a mistake to assume your wardrobe must be entirely bland and impersonal

Making yourself invisible is no way to enhance your personal impact. Being distinctive and stylish should be perfectly possible, even within the limitations set by the conventions surrounding you. Look for creative ways to make your clothes really reflect who you are and not solely how others apparently want you to be. Apart from clothes, your demeanour also consists of how you carry yourself, including grooming, your general expression – do you smile a lot or mainly frown – how you walk, your general bearing and your social manners.

Getting help

Not everyone has a natural flair for clothes and style. The only thing worse than not having it is not having it and not knowing you do not have it! As with all areas of self-awareness, the great secret is really not a secret at all – get honest feedback.

To obtain feedback on your clothes and style there are plenty of specialists around from colour experts to personal shoppers in large department stores, from fashion and style advisers to one-to-one coaches who focus on the whole area of personal impact, including working on appearance. You will find some useful sources at the Charisma Effect website (www. charisma-effect.com).

The social sins

A famous charismatic stage and film star once invited a young unknown actress to dinner. Not only did her guest fail to appear, but neglected to apologise or explain her absence. Some days later, the two women unexpectedly met at the Museum of Modern Art in New York. 'I think I was invited to your house to dinner last Thursday night', the young woman began. 'Oh, yes?' replied the star, 'Did you come?'

Manners may no longer quite top the bill for success these days, but they remain an important factor in affecting your demeanour. Don't reserve your best behaviour for special occasions. You can't have two sets of manners, one for those you admire and want to impress and another for those whom you consider unimportant. For a strong demeanour they need to be the same for everyone.

Since manners are simply artificial rules, they can be broken under the right circumstances. For example, in England people usually expect men to remove their hats indoors. However, if wearing a stylish hat is your personal fashion statement then you may be able to get away with this, using it to build your particular personal impact.

Here are seven common deadly social sins.

1 Failing to say thank you when someone has shown you an act of kindness.
2 Sitting badly in meetings, including rocking back and forth in your chair.

3 Being overly familiar with someone without permission.
4 Not treating people with respect.
5 Touching objects or people without direct encouragement.
6 Continuously interrupting or loudly dominating the airwaves.
7 Disparaging someone in front of someone who matters to them.

The point about manners is they need to be appropriate, showing respect for your audience.

Personal grooming

Now let's get really personal. I mean the territory that only your best friends or someone you fully trust dares enter.

Brian was sent on the road by his company to learn about the basics of selling and distribution. His job was to visit small retail chemists and take restocking orders. In one shop, after talking at length to the owner, the latter politely invited him to come to the back room, where spare stock was piled to the ceiling.

In the privacy of this unpretentious space the owner said quietly: 'Brian, has anyone ever told you that you have extremely bad breath?' Brian's eyes widened in horror; no one had ever said anything like that, ever. 'Well you do, young man, and I urge you to do something about it. It could do you lots of harm on your way up the ladder.' To his credit, Brian responded with gratitude to this feedback and immediately visited his dentist to sort out the problem, which turned out to be a gum infection.

When Gordon Brown was chancellor, press photographs of his severely bitten nails went round the world. True, it did not stop him becoming prime minister, but it weakened the image of an otherwise apparently confident man in charge of the nation's finances.

To check your image, do the Personal grooming killers work out opposite.

Personal grooming killers work out

Take an honest look at yourself and only tick the boxes if you are sure.

		✓
BREATH	Is your breath fresh?	
	Would anyone actually tell you if it was not?	
HAIR	Is your hair washed, ungreasy and in a modern style?	
	No wisps trying to cover up bald pates?	
TEETH	In reasonable order; fresh looking?	
FACIAL HAIR	Carefully attended to, including ears and nostrils?	
	No unruly, unflattering, untrimmed, unshaven areas?	
CHEW GUM	You don't!	
CLEANLINESS	Are your nails, face, hands, all visible areas well scrubbed?	
NAILS	Are these well-cared for, not bitten or chewed?	
DANDRUFF	None in evidence (there is no excuse these days)?	
SKIN	Fresh and healthy looking, not sallow, flaky or greying?	

We are so used to our own bodies that it can be hard to recognise when something begins to affect our personal impact adversely. This really is best-friend territory and it is worth asking someone you trust to tell you frankly whether you are experiencing any of the personal grooming killers.

> this really is best-friend territory

My colleague, Michael Maynard, who has helped countless people develop their potential and their charisma, argues that the key point about personal grooming is, 'It's about care. Do you look as if you take care, and do you look cared for?'

Posture

Avril, an experienced headteacher and assistant director of education, kept applying for jobs as a director of education in large English local councils. She was constantly shortlisted for interviews, yet kept failing to win the high-level job she wanted.

Personal coaching revealed her habit of entering the interview room with her head down and slouching – it was as if she was apologising for even being there. Her mental attitude, partly influenced by her negative posture, ran along the lines of, 'I wonder if they will appoint me this time.' The combination of the two directly affected her demeanour and reduced her Charisma Effect.

In one-to-one coaching, Avril learned to walk tall, with head held high. She began entering the room while imagining she was *already* a director of education and was attending merely to answer a few questions, using her expertise and experience. Transformed, Avril used the learning at her next assistant director interview and was duly appointed.

As a child, Queen Victoria was trained to keep her chin up by the presence of a prickly sprig of holly under her collar. The postures of Elvis, Nijinsky, David Bowie, John Wayne and Prince all contributed to their particular Charisma Effect. Even though we tend to pay less attention to the importance of posture these days, it can still directly affect demeanour.

You can gain from some outside feedback, either in a one-to-one coaching session or in a workshop dealing with postural and other issues. For example, watching yourself come through a door to meet a group of strangers can prove a revelation.

If you spend hours hunched over a computer, it is a fair guess your posture will suffer. We see many people with heads poked forward and walking badly due to excessive screen time. Most people think standing straight consists of tensing the back, heaving the chest in and up and pulling one's head towards their chest. This is not so. The spine has two natural curves that you need to maintain: from the base of your head to your shoulders and the curve from the upper back to the base of the spine. Consider learning the Alexander Technique with a qualified teacher. This proven method prevents stoop and unnecessary muscle tension. It helps regain natural posture and adds a quality of ease to the way you move and work.

If you feel pain, especially back pain, when trying to attain a good posture or suffer from back, neck or pelvic injuries, do not attempt to correct these yourself. This could cause further damage. Contact your doctor or visit an Alexander Technique teacher before trying to tamper with your alignment.

Posture work out

- When standing straight up, make sure that your weight is evenly distributed on your feet, both forwards and sideways. It might feel as if you are leaning too far forward, and look stupid, but you don't.
- Push your shoulders forward, then bring them straight up, then straight back, then down. Feel good? If your shoulders feel slightly stiff or tense you may have unnecessary muscle tension.
- If your head hangs forward you cannot be properly aligned. Keep your head at a level that allows you to look directly ahead without having to turn your eyes up. If this causes tension in your neck you are in need of some retraining.
  - Align ears with shoulders.
  - Raise both arms out to sides at shoulder height.
  - Hold for a slow count of 10.
  - Slowly lower arms to sides, counting to 10 as you lower.
  - Do 10 repetitions, constantly checking your alignment! If 10 reps are too many to start, do as many as you can. You should at least feel a slight fatigue in the shoulder muscles.

- Be a penguin. While waiting for a web page to load, toast to pop up or the microwave to beep, place elbows at your side and touch your shoulders with your hands. Keeping your hands on your shoulders and your ears aligned, raise both elbows sideways, count one, two and lower them back to your waist, count one, two. Do as many reps as your wait allows. You'll be surprised how much exercise fits into 30 seconds.

'To live is not just to survive but to thrive, with some passion, some compassion, some humour and a little bit of style!'

Maya Angelou, writer

Part 3

Chemistry

Create that special attraction

Chapter 10

Chemistry

'It's more important to click with people than to click the shutter,' remarked the father of photojournalism and *Life* magazine's star picture maker Alfred Einsentaedt. He should know having worked with numerous highly demanding celebs from Sophia Loren, Ernest Hemingway, and Joseph Goebbels, to that master of personal chemistry Bill Clinton when president.

Clarifying your aim and being yourself (see earlier sections) help build the foundations of charisma. Personal chemistry provides the catalyst. It transforms these elements into a magnetic force that makes you stand out and be memorable. It is the vital, invisible agent, able to change everything, and sometimes everybody.

The entertainment world obsesses over personal chemistry and its link to charisma. For explosive chemical reactions both on screen and privately, Greta Garbo and John Gilbert, Marlene Dietrich and director Von Sternberg, and Richard Burton and Elizabeth Taylor set the pace in the last century.

More recently, Tom Cruise and Katie Holmes, Brad Pitt and Angelina Jolie, Julia Roberts and Richard Gere, and many others, continue to precipitate floods of comment, gossip and analysis about their positive personal chemistry.

Sometimes the stories show the reverse. One of the most widely publicised was when the previously strong chemistry between the board of Hewlett Packard and their charismatic CEO Carly Fiorina broke down spectacularly. They summarily fired her in 2005.

Occasionally people succeed not so much because of their charisma but despite it. The film *The Social Network* portrayed Facebook founder Mark Zuckerberg as an unsmiling, insecure, obsessed young man, with zero personality or ability to create personal chemistry. Many bitter ex-employees and former friends say the film is highly realistic. Videos of him texting madly on his phone, while walking around town oblivious of those around him, hardly show someone bubbling with charisma. Perhaps that hardly matters if you become the richest young entrepreneur in the entire world.

We cannot observe the chemistry underpinning charisma. It involves invisible events, including arousal of the sympathetic nervous system, rising blood pressure, weakness in the knees, pleasurable feelings, joy, a lightness of being and so on.

Though chemistry and its consequences between human beings remain out of sight, we surely notice their absence. People say, for example, 'there was no chemistry between us', meaning nothing special happened. Describing the actor Kenneth Branagh in 2011, a critic commented, 'Whatever charisma and magnetism are, Branagh does not possess or exude them.'

Do you insist on always being in control or like to micro manage? Do you constantly want things your own way? If so, the whole idea of personal chemistry will probably feel frustrating since you cannot easily measure or control it, nor be entirely sure it is happening.

Personal chemistry sounds so touchy-feely it seems a throwback to the days of Dale Carnegie and his decades-old best seller, *How to Win Friends and Influence People*. Based on psychological research and practical work in helping people actually make a stronger personal impact, there are some practical principles for stimulating personal chemistry. Once again they revolve around experiments, trial and error and a readiness to learn as you go along.

Chemical reaction

Long ago humans mastered the art of lighting a fire. The formula was simple and learnable: heat, fuel and air. Without any one of these, the result becomes an embarrassing mess. The chemistry of charisma is more complicated; not only is each situation unique, no one can be sure of the exact mix of ingredients or which will be the most critical.

For example, how important is 'charm' in creating personal chemistry, and, if it matters, should you acquire it? The modern *Oxford English Dictionary* even defines charisma as 'Compelling attractiveness or charm that can inspire devotion in others.'

Whatever the esteemed *OED* says, charm is not the same as charisma. Charm seduces, pacifies, assures and even promotes complacency. A notorious charmer of the nineteenth century was George 'Beau' Brummell, whose limited charisma was apparent to those around him. Yet with his ultra laidback manner, he flattered and induced others to follow his every sartorial whim. For a brief period, through his highly personal influence on the susceptible Prince of Wales, Brummell became the arbiter of style and fashion.

Charm is far more superficial than charisma, yet can be tricky to establish. Actor Cary Grant, who on screen once personified charm, reportedly complained in frustration, 'Even I want to be Cary Grant.' Actors Sean Connery, Roger Moore and Pierce Brosnan each fairly painlessly imbued James Bond with an indelible quota of charm, while for all his good looks Daniel Craig struggled to match them on the charm front and, say his critics, in the charisma department too.

> charm is far more superficial than charisma

Charisma inspires, enlivens, excites, delights and promotes action. In contrast, when charmers leave the room they take their effect with them. The departure of those with strong charisma, though, creates an emotional vacuum, leaving others longing for their return. In other words, their Charisma Effect is sustained. Charm may indeed dazzle your dinner guests, but only charisma will enthral a 20,000-seater stadium full of strangers.

Charm is obviously a desirable human characteristic, yet is not essential to creating a powerful and lasting impression. Alone it is seldom enough to create the right chemistry. To contribute to charisma it usually must be part of some other substantial behaviour, such as being a strong character.

Unfortunately, charm is also rather too easy to switch on and off. For example, Rupert Murdoch can exude personal charm, but his 'natural state', says his biographer, Michael Wolff, in *Vanity Fair*, is 'war'. Amin and Hitler could do charming and when combined with their strong character certainly had a powerful Charisma Effect. On the other hand, while both Ghandi and Mother Teresa possessed a certain charisma, many commented more on their extraordinary ability to turn on the charm when they needed it.

Underlining the limited role charm may play in creating the chemistry of charisma is the fact that we may even dislike some charismatics. By most standards, for example, Mrs Thatcher had a degree of charisma, yet in public sorely lacked charm.

Personal chemistry created by charisma stems from a unique blend of:

- Aim (see Chapter 2)
- Being yourself (see Part 2)
- Smiling (see Chapter 11)
- Eye contact and body language (see Chapter 12)
- Energy
- Rapport

Unique to you, that is; the mix would be different for someone else. This is why you need to keep learning, trying different approaches until you become satisfied with the impact your charisma makes.

Energy

Martin Luther King, Elvis Presley and Muhammad Ali all lit up a room through their presence and high level of energy. Like starting a fire, personal chemistry invariably involves a commitment of energy, directed at an audience. Putting it more bluntly, you must fuel your charisma by making an effort, investing yourself in the process, expending energy.

According to scientists, each of us is a bundle of pulsating energy that constantly interacts with our surroundings. Charismatic people exude and attract energy, creating a life force that partly explains the secret of 'personal magnetism'.

charismatic people exude and attract energy

The energy we are talking about is both physical and also internal. Internal energy is an inner force that feeds the external drive that so many charismatics exhibit. With practice you can learn to cultivate your internal energy.

External energy spreads your internal energy outwards. It affects others positively, creating a 'feel-good factor' that is both compelling and memorable.

When your energy output takes a positive form it makes other people feel energised too. Consequently they feel valued and productive, and they respond even more strongly to the source – your charisma. While you cannot actually see positive energy, we recognise it in action when we see it. We say someone has passion, commitment, excitement, enthusiasm, determination, ebullience, and even humour.

Gifted orators rely on conveying their message not just through their words but also through their positive energy. The combination can be so compelling that it inspires listeners, sometimes seeming to literally 'blow people's minds', reducing their critical faculties. They may become almost mesmerised by the impact. How else do you explain, for example, the famous ability of performance coach Anthony Robbins who regularly persuades his enraptured audiences to walk across burning coals?

There is also a difference between male and female energy and its impact on people. Female energy tends to be intuitive, receptive, nurturing. When charismatic people use this kind of energy, it can have a strong emotional impact. Both men and women have the ability to develop and use this kind of energy, though women are often more at home with it.

Likewise, male energy tends to be the strong, forceful side of ourselves. When charismatic people use this kind of energy it makes things happen, gets things done and is strongly results-orientated. Although more strongly associated with men, women can often make it a powerful part of their charisma.

Those who trigger a strong personal chemistry around them will usually be adept at balancing both the female and male forms of energy that we experience as magnetism or charisma.

What conclusions for action can we draw from this evidence?

First, explore ways to build your internal energy. While internal energy has been known for centuries, the process of generating it is less familiar in the West. However, the three principles underpinning it are gradually becoming more familiar. They are:

- Regulating the body – through posture.
- Regulating the breath – through, for example, controlled abdominal breathing.
- Regulating the mind – through mental discipline.

For instance, meditation, yoga, Tai Chi, Qui Gong, Alexander Technique and some other martial arts disciplines such as Karate can be enjoyable ways to discover how to do these systematically.

Start building internal energy

1 Sitting

Action: Sit on the floor; relax your body; breathe naturally; don't try to think of anything, just be attentive to what is happening.

Time: Take five minutes each day.

2 Breathing

Action: Count your breaths from one to 10; after counting to 10, repeat the process. Allow the process of breathing in and out to slow down naturally.

Time: Do it for one minute for a few days then gradually expand to five minutes.

3 Standing

Action: Stand upright with feet parallel and a few inches apart.

Let your arms hang by your sides. Close your eyes.

Mentally 'visit' each of your limbs, each foot and hand, then each shoulder, your neck and your face.

Review whether the muscles are tense or relaxed.

'Invite' tense muscles to let go and relax.

Time: Take two minutes to start with and expand to five minutes.

It may seem you are doing very little to create internal energy, but these kinds of exercises are a great way to begin sharpening your charisma.

Secondly, be willing to expend and direct your energy outwards towards others. For example, pursue a cause, stand up for what you feel matters, speak for those with no voice, offer an opinion, and show a level of commitment to which others invariably respond.

Thirdly, value your own energy and do not waste it.

Rapport

Adam Levine, lead singer and guitarist for the pop group Maroon 5, has a tremendous rapport with his fans, 'but it took him eight years to develop,' says his mother. 'At his first performances, he performed with his back to the audience!'

Rapport is about building a relationship. Oprah Winfrey, the American talk show host, thrives on building a close rapport with her audience. Her chosen way is through telling stories and self-revelation. Among her favourite early tales is that in the past she took drugs, suffered rape as a child and, while struggling with her ballooning weight, once ate a jumbo package of hot-dog buns, drenched in maple syrup.

Learning how to generate rapport is no different from acquiring any other skill. If you are not a natural tennis player, both practice and coaching can often help. Similarly, guidance on rapport building and experimentation can help you improve at it. A good starting point is to devote far more attention to the audience than you have done previously. (See below.)

We each build relationships with people in our own way; it is an art, not a science. To encourage the creation of rapport you can use some or all of the techniques listed in the box opposite.

Rapport builders

- **Connect** – look for areas where you have something in common with your audience.
- **Sensitivity** – assess other people's state of mind by watching for a mixture of verbal and non-verbal cues.
- **Empathy** – imagine walking in their shoes to understand their situation and what they are experiencing.
- **Respect** – avoid making people feel bad, or demeaned in some way.
- **Physicality** – matching or mirroring someone's gestures affects how they relate to you; works best when you show interest in them as people.
- **Language** – carefully chosen words and phrases affect people's emotions and promote rapport, for example paying a genuine compliment.
- **Questions** – intelligence queries give someone the chance to shine; for example, offer open-ended ones that encourage them to talk and share interesting information.
- **Support** – offer unconditional help or information to signal you want to build the relationship.
- **Stories** – personal stories work because listeners feel more than just entertained, they see you in a fresh light.

Ways to communicate your empathy

- **Avoid being judgemental:** make it clear you are not evaluating or criticising the other person, just trying to understand.
- **Listen attentively, with concern:** show your involvement with suitable facial expressions and physical gestures.
- **Reflect back:** convey to the other person the feelings you think they are experiencing; check the accuracy of your perceptions.
- **Use self-disclosure:** share your understanding through offering some personal information, but avoid putting the focus back on yourself.

- **Make room for others to speak:** rather than filling the silence with your own thoughts or feelings. Empathy is often just giving the other person room to reflect and share.
- **Check back:** watch for clues your response is accurate, such as the person giving a nod, or a phrase such as 'that's right' or 'exactly'.
- **Be patient:** empathy and being in a hurry do not mix; there are no short cuts.

Empathy works best from a spirit of curiosity, a sort of deliberate ignorance. Rather than trying to assume what another person thinks or feels, or even means, you show you are genuinely interested through intense listening, full attention, appropriate body language and encouragement that in effect says 'tell me more'.

Attention

Meeting Bill Clinton, a UK colleague remarked that the ex-President 'always makes me feel he'd flown the Atlantic for the sole purpose of talking to me.'

Give someone your complete, undivided attention and like Clinton you will be using one of the most flattering and magnetic tools at your disposal to build rapport. Full attention means that the audience – whether one person or many – entirely fills your vision. It is like donning horse blinkers to shut out all distractions.

In talking with individuals it means no peering over the other person's shoulder to see what else might be happening, no half an ear listening to a nearby conversation, no fiddling with a laptop or mobile. Instead, you remain focused, laser-like, on the person with whom you are engaging.

With groups, it means watching continuously for signs that tell you what the audience needs from you and then giving it to them. Rather than just pushing your own agenda, full attention involves constant scanning, observing and analysing.

In rapport building, complete attention involves far more than looking fixedly at people's faces. Certainly, you maintain regular eye contact, smile and use sound body language – see later chapters – however, complete attention implies varied actions that you can practise and master.

For example, you look interested, use and remember names, listen actively, talk about interests, treat the person as important, accept and build, make the other person look good, avoid making the other person wrong, and so on.

Look interested

To look interested you need to *be* interested! This partly explains how many successful people rapidly establish a strong charisma. If only briefly, they convey a genuine, intense, and rewarding interest in you.

> to look interested you need to *be* interested!

Being interested in someone can feel a struggle, especially if the other person makes it hard to understand what is special about them. Yet dig deep enough and everyone reveals something curious about themselves, such as their intentions, experience, opinions and desires. Charismatic people expend precious energy finding out about others, assuming there is something worthwhile to be discovered.

Certain signals confirm your interest in someone. For example, you nod at appropriate moments, lean forward silently, make encouraging sounds such as 'uhuh, mmm, ahh', look thoughtful and so on. Small gestures like these may be hardly noticed at the time, yet they often separate the person who creates personal chemistry from someone who does not. (See for example lingering eye contact, in Chapter 12.)

Use and remember names

It's said that hearing one's name spoken by other people is the sweetest sound in the world. In building rapport, people with charisma know the importance of using and remembering names. How good are you at this game? Are you like so many people, simply bad at remembering names and wish you could do better?

Brain expert and writer Tony Buzan, who organises world memory championships, explains, 'The main reason why people forget, is that they haven't paid attention in the first place.' That particularly applies to people's names. We simply fail to make enough effort to be able to recall a name, even when we have heard it only a few moments ago.

Saying 'I have a bad memory for names' is therefore something of a cop out. It is a convenient way of implying that forgetfulness is somehow inevitable, as if you are missing the gene for recalling names.

In fact, unless you have an actual medical condition, you can certainly improve your recall for names using some easy, tried and tested ways such as those shown in the box below. The real question is: how serious are you about improving your charisma? If you are determined to do so then, sorry, but you may need to commit to getting better at name recall!

'We had a lot in common. I loved him and he loved him.'

Shelley Winters, actress, in *Bittersweet*

Seven ways to recall people's names

- **Desire:** You must genuinely want to remember the person's name.
- **Stop and listen:** Too often, we meet someone and immediately launch into another conversation.

- **Use it:** Do this several times during the conversation. Don't overdo the repetition; more than three times in a five-minute conversation would sound forced.
- **Verify:** Unless the person has introduced himself to you, check the name this person would like you to use.
- **Link it:** Rather than thinking of the name as a sound, link it directly to a memorable, preferably bizarre image.

One president of the United States amazed his many staff by always remembering their names. His method was to visualise the person's name boldly printed on their forehead.

Samantha – the panther, sexy and black

Jack – climbing a bright red bean stalk

Thomas – the front of a Tank Engine

Joshua – blowing down the walls of Jericho

Grace – a gazelle, gracefully lolloping along

Ruby – stuck inside a giant ruby and trying to get out

- **Write:** Note down the person's name; if it's inconvenient, simply imagine yourself jotting it down, even creating the feeling of actually writing with tiny hidden hand movements, while saying the name silently in your head. Later, actually jot down the person's name three times, while picturing their face.
- **Face files:** On meeting someone for the first time, find something striking about their facial appearance. It could be their nose, large forehead, or lips. Ignore hair or glasses as these can change over time.

Say their name to yourself, along with their facial characteristic. For example, 'John with the long nose; Peter with the narrow lips; Mike with the dimple on his chin; Melanie with green eyes.'

Listen actively

One day in 2001, film director Roman Polanski called Robert Evans, the producer and a recent author. He complained he had been in a car accident, destroying his new Mercedes. 'What happened?' Evans asked.

'I was driving down the Champs Elysées listening to your new book,' Polanski explained, 'and I was laughing so hard I crashed into a tree!'

It is best not to be doing something else at the same time as listening attentively. For example, you cannot expect to generate much rapport while talking with someone if you continue to tap at a keyboard, check for messages on your mobile, scribble distractedly in a notebook and fiddle with a desk toy.

When listening actively, make sure you have a clear purpose in mind. For example, you may choose to stay alert for obtaining specific information, to solve a problem, to understand, to be able to encourage. You may also decide to be on the look out for revealing phrases, tell-tale emotive words, a particular tone of voice, pace of speech, particular speech patterns, metaphors, and use of images. Any of these may tell you what the person is thinking or feeling and provides clues as to how you might respond.

when listening actively, make sure you have a clear purpose in mind

Active listening work out

1 Face the speaker – show your attentiveness, sit up straight or lean forward slightly.

2 Maintain comfortable eye contact – avoid letting your gaze wander to other people or other activities taking place.

3 Minimise external and internal distractions – turn off your laptop and mobile; ask the speaker and other listeners to do the same.
4 Acknowledge – when they speak murmur 'uh-huh' and 'um-hmm', and nod. Raise your eyebrows. Offer comments such as, 'Really,' or 'Interesting'.
5 Focus solely on what the speaker says – try not to think about what you are wanting to say next.
6 Watch for non-verbal clues – notice what the speaker does, as much as what he or she says.
7 Keep an open mind – avoid making assumptions about what the person is thinking, or what they will say next.
8 Avoid offering gratuitous advice – just assume the person needs to talk it out, until you get asked a specific question suggesting help is needed.
9 Listen for key words or phrases – these are the ones that suggest feelings or emotion.
10 Engage – ask questions for clarification without seeming to conduct an inquisition.
11 Reflect back – try playing the mental game of never offering your own view until you have first summarised aloud your understanding of what the other person has just said. Use reflecting phrases such as: 'You said', 'You mentioned', 'You suggested before', 'You described'.
12 Do not interrupt – with practice you will get better at this. Even when there is a pause, hold back your contribution and wait to confirm the speaker has really finished.

Talk about interests

As people get to know each other and build a relationship they exchange increasingly personal information. When you ask someone what interests them you will often tap into their enthusiasm or commitment. One way to start the ball rolling is by sharing some of your own current work or social interests and see if they land with the other person.

Treat the person as important

People like to feel valued and respected. When done well, absolute attention conveys this. For example, you take what they say seriously, giving it obvious thought. Even if you disagree with their point of view, make it clear they are entitled to their opinion. Ask them about their views, problems they see, reservations they have.

Somewhere along the way, you will locate a cross-over point where you find a mutual agenda which encourages the natural chemistry between you.

Accept and build

The essence of Accept and Build is taking what someone says and working with it constructively. You keep adding value to their suggestions, or to what they have said. Without having to agree with them, for example, you may choose to take the idea in a different direction.

A particularly good way to trigger Accept and Build is to keep using the phrase 'Yes and...' in response to what someone says, rather than 'Yes but...'.

Accept and build in action

'Why don't we shut the office and spend an afternoon together on the river?'

'Yes and... we could also each bring an item of food to create a team meal.'

'Yes and... someone could bring an mp3 player with a speaker for some music.'

'Yes and... we could ask people in advance what music they want.'

'I think it's time we had a new brochure.'

'Yes and... it could also be the right time to re-do our website.'

'Yes and... while we're doing that why don't we....'

'The office is starting to look a mess again, time we had another collective tidying session.'

'Yes and… let's hire someone to do it for us!'

'Yes and… I could organise a waste collection on that day too.'

'Yes and… while I personally like the mess, I'll bring some music to cheer you up while you're doing it!'

The most obvious example of Accept and Build in action is during brain-storming sessions. If well run, they leave criticism till later. In the early stages, everyone makes suggestions and there is continuous encouragement to build on each other's contribution.

Use Accept and Build as part of your natural response to people and they will see you in a positive, rather than a negative light, someone with a strong charisma who values what they say.

Make the other person look good

This builds rapport by showing you care about someone's success or achievements. No matter how apparently small or insignificant these may be, you make an opportunity to show you value their specific contribution. In doing so it makes you part of their success. For example:

- In a team meeting when someone asks a question, you take the opportunity to make them look good by saying: 'That's a really good question,' 'You always get to the root of things,' or 'I bet that's given us quite a lot of food for thought'.
- When introducing a client to a colleague: 'This is Mary who runs the customer care department, she has an absolute passion for keeping customers happy.'

Making the other person look good is rather like having a public love affair that stays firmly in the work setting and never carries over into private life.

Reciprocity

When people get on with each other, there is genuine give and take. Without it, little of substance happens between human beings. Assume the other person wants to build a relationship with you, and use the basic principles of reciprocity:

- To gain attention, *be attentive.*
- To become interesting, *be interested.*
- To be understood, seek to understand.
- Avoid making the other person wrong.

This is similar to the earlier action of making the person look good. Rather than contradicting them, finding fault or suggesting they have got something wrong, instead offer a new perspective, an alternative view, or a different interpretation.

For example, suppose someone in a presentation shows a slide with a percentage column that seems to add up wrongly. Rather than pointing out their mistake and making them feel small, you find a different way; for example, 'Does this column add up to more than 100 per cent due to rounding errors perhaps?'

Name it

Share your view of what might be happening in the moment. Invite others' opinion about it too. For example:

- 'Does anyone else besides me feel a need for a break?'
- 'Seems we're going over the same ground, shall we move on?'
- 'You sound frustrated with my response, shall we talk about it?'
- 'I sense quite a bit of confusion about this.'

When you name what is going on you reduce its negative power and increase its positive power. For example, when you say, 'I am having a terrific time here' you are inviting them to feel that way too.

People with charisma often use superlatives in their speech as part of naming what is happening. 'That's wonderful!' 'Tremendous.' 'Wow!' 'How exciting.' 'Terrific to meet you', 'I am *so* impressed.' This works when this is done from the heart, conveying a genuine feeling of pleasure, excitement, understanding and so on. It is also quite seductive.

Chemistry in action

The chemistry that charisma creates is rather like cooking in the dark. Even with the recipe and knowing the ingredients, you still have to locate them for yourself and mix them in the right way for your particular charisma cake.

People with a strong charisma invest energy and skill in building a strong relationship with their audience. This may include using a whole range of interpersonal behaviours that are both learnable and capable of being practised. Some are more intangible than others, but nearly all are fuelled by energy and personal insight or self-awareness.

Part 4

Digging deeper into charisma

This fourth part looks at three specific areas of charisma that link what it means to Be Yourself and the chemistry of charisma.

- Smiling and charisma
- Eye contact and body language
- Leadership and charisma

There are practical actions in each of these areas you can take to strengthen your charisma and the impression you make on people.

Chapter 11

Smiling and charisma

Top comedian Michael McIntyre wears a smile almost as wide as his rather chunky body. Grinning relentlessly, he paces up and down the stage telling his amusing stories. With a national tour sold out almost 18 months in advance, McIntyre's curious delivery and unique style wins over people of all ages.

His ready smile has an impact because he seems to be enjoying himself so enormously. He clearly loves every minute of being on stage, being in contact with his rapt audience. Combined with restless energy his visible smile says, 'I'm having fun doing this.'

He rarely needs to fake or force a smile since it is an intrinsic part of his obvious charisma. For McIntyre and many others, smiling builds their charisma. Yet there remain many questions about how it works.

For instance, why do we smile in the first place? Is smiling essential for charisma? What is an inner smile? Can we tinker with our smile for a stronger charisma impact? And perhaps inevitably, does a fake smile help charisma?

Why do we smile?

For millennia, smiling has played a vital part in human development and in public perceptions of charisma.

Originally, it had limited purposes, enabling us to communicate with others at a distance, for example when hunting or confronting potential enemies. According to Dacher Keltner, a psychology professor at the University of California in Berkeley, we humans can detect the average smile from 300 feet away, even if it lasts only three seconds. 'In that time you can reveal much more of yourself than you ever intended. Sometimes you give away big facts.' Later it began playing an important role in influencing others, in persuasion and affecting how people felt.

Smiles are in fact a shorthand way of communicating all kinds of messages. Presumably, this is why researchers know of at least 18 smile variations that we can call on to make our point.

Like yawning, smiling is catching and this has important implications for building charisma. The latest brain research identifies a specific type of neuron that for the first time explains why we smile back. When you see someone else smile, a 'mirror' neuron fires in your brain to copy it and consequently you return the smile, almost without thinking. An Indian saying it expresses it more poetically: 'The smile that you give out comes back to you.'

smiling is catching and this has important implications for building charisma

Mirror neurons, among the most important recent discoveries in neuroscience, confirm why smiling a lot can have a profound impact, affecting others even without their realising it. Professor Wiseman, a psychologist at the University of Hertfordshire, in the UK, with an international reputation for research into luck, deception, the paranormal and humour, explains that, 'You're unaware you're mimicking this person, although you know they make you feel happy.'

'It's emotional contagion,' is how brain expert and University of Florida associate professor Amir Erez puts it.

Given the large number of different smiles one can use, which one makes the most impact when we are being charismatic? 'The best smile is the felt smile,' says Paul Ekman, professor of psychology at the University of California and possibly the world's greatest authority on smiles. A felt smile is one that comes from your emotions, driven by genuine feelings.

The smile facts

- We have a face built to smile. It hides some 3000 muscles that in combination create our varied expressions; many of them will be fleeting and hardly noticeable, except at an unconscious level.
- It is easier to smile than to frown. It takes 43 facial muscles to create a frown, and only 17 to generate a smile, although you can use up to 53 for a cheesy grin.
- You are born with the smiling instinct; you did not learn to do it. Even blind babies smile.
- Women smile more than men do – could that be why they live longer?
- Research recognises 18 particular types of smile, used in various social situations.
- Studies suggest if you smile, people will regard you as more sincere, attractive, sociable, and competent, hence its contribution to charisma.
- Due to a chemical release of serotonin in the brain, smiling actually makes you feel better.
- It is not essential to smile in creating a strong charisma, but it certainly helps.
- Smiling triggers an uncontrolled brain response in others, causing them to mirror back the smile.
- Smiles that work best come from within. Forced smiles can quickly be detected by most people.

Is smiling essential for charisma?

'And Anita's smile I remember. I mean, her wonderful smile in those days promised everything.'

Marianne Faithful on Anita Pallenberg, Italian-born actor, model, and fashion designer and romantic partner of Keith Richards of the Rolling Stones

In many instances, charisma and smiling prove to be virtually inseparable. It is not that smiling is essential for a strong personal impact, but it certainly seems to help, especially when you clearly have an authentic smile.

Say what you will about Barack Obama, and what he represents, the man does a great and convincing smile, like his predecessor Bill Clinton. Smiling is patently an essential feature of his charisma and few would dispute that. Yet how essential is it for creating charisma?

Smiling only partly explains the formidable impact both he and Clinton achieve when working the crowds. Clinton in particular does not merely smile, he is ecstatic. For him, affecting those around him is not a duty; it is what he enjoys most.

Sometimes even those with Extreme Charisma may lack a natural smile – see Chapter 1. So, clearly it is perfectly possible to develop a strong charisma without constantly emitting beaming smiles. In fact, charisma sometimes works best when smiling is more of a rarity, a sudden sunburst that lights up the surroundings.

charisma sometimes works best when smiling is more of a rarity

As already noted, smiling is a highly practical form of communication and currently we associate it with radiating confidence, energy, and pleasure at being with people. Such associations enhance charisma, since people both recognise the signs, and find themselves automatically responding.

Unsurprisingly, people with a powerful charisma devote a lot of time to smiling because it shares their happiness and spreads a feel-good factor. It is part of how they promote personal chemistry, whether showing empathy or building rapport – see Chapter 10.

Smile workout – 1

If you are someone who forgets to smile, your smile muscles can literally start to atrophy. Give yourself some practice at getting back in touch with your smile.

1 Take a long look at your smile in the mirror – at least five consecutive minutes.
2 Make careful notes of what you see. For example, do you have a strictly pasted-on look or do your eyes seem to twinkle too?
3 Find some pictures of you smiling. Even if you hate having your picture taken, you can almost certainly track down at least one where you look great, with a naturally contagious smile.
4 Use that picture to have a good look at what your face is doing.
5 Return to your mirror and practise that particular smile, paying attention to how it feels, so that you can replicate it without looking in the mirror.
6 Start a Smile Journal. Record moments that put a real smile on your face, moments of joy and laughter, no matter how small or briefly.
7 Start with just one moment and relive the emotion at the time, bring it to life by recalling it in detail.
8 If you have trouble filling the journal, it tells you why you need to put smiling back on your daily personal agenda.

Although smiling certainly can help strengthen your charisma, it works best when it comes from within – the **Inner Smile**

What's an inner smile?

'Her smile was not meant to be seen by anyone and served its whole purpose in being smiled.'

Maria Rilke, *Journal of my Other Self*

As noted earlier, there is physical evidence that when you smile it releases certain chemicals in the brain, including the feel-good one of serotonin. These cause bodily changes, including relaxation and a sense of well-being. It does not seem to matter whether your face actually smiles or you only smile mentally, both the act of smiling and thinking about smiling can be good for you.

Nor is there anything flaky or weird about an inner smile, sometimes described as smiling from the heart rather than consciously instructing your face muscles to move. It is true you cannot detect an inner smile with any kind of an instrument, apart perhaps from a lowering of blood pressure.

Yet some of the sanest people on Earth know their inner smile exists. They value it and, consciously or otherwise, practise it assiduously. Many with an enviable charisma rely on their inner smile to create or trigger an authentic, outwardly visible smile.

So, an inner smile can be important in both affecting how you smile physically and can be an essential part of charisma. Since you cannot actually see an inner smile, how would you go about finding yours? Start with 'looking inside you'. That is, invest time in growing your self-awareness; becoming more alert as to how you are feeling in the moment.

Finding your inner smile is only the start though; the next step is extending it outwards, so it affects situations where you need your charisma. This translates as both an actual facial smile that people perceive as genuine, and affects your demeanour and attitude towards people.

Polishing your inner smile

You can do this sitting on an airplane, stuck in traffic, waiting in a shopping line, getting ready for a meeting, preparing a presentation, taking an office break and so on.

- Be still, with eyes open or closed.
- Accept and acknowledge where you are.
- Use your memory of some past joyful experience to get in touch with feeling serene. It could be seeing a smiling baby, or being somewhere that made you feel at one with the world.
- Feel the energy moving through your body, radiating outwards, downwards, upwards, inwards.
- Search for a feeling of a smile, a faint hint of smiling from somewhere around your heart, and definitely from inside. You may even find it helpful to place your hand over your heart.
- Lift the corners of your mouth slightly without forcing them. Allow them to turn upwards naturally, as your inner smile gently permeates your face. Feel it soften your eyes.
- As you contact your smile, allow it to have a life of its own, and feel the good feeling. Rather than forcing your smile to happen, let it emerge naturally.
- Notice how the thought of smiling encourages your face to smile, how even thinking about smiling seems to trigger more smiling.
- Stay quietly with your inner smile, enjoying the moment. Allow the feeling to stay activated for as many minutes as you can.
- Gently move out into the world, smiling from the inside, radiating it outwards.

You always have time to practise your inner smile.

Activate your inner smile when you want to make a strong impression on people, when you need to use your full charisma.

Tinkering with our smile

In our image-conscious age there is now a whole industry devoted to improving how people smile, whether through altering teeth, noses, hairline, and filling in wrinkles and propping up sagging jaws.

Realising that a better smile could help them make a stronger impact, some notable celebs have spent heavily on artificial enhancements. Like moths to a flame the big spenders on smile enhancements have allegedly included Tom Cruise at £15k, Catherine Zeta-Jones, David Bowie and Nicole Kidman each at £20k, and Michael Douglas and Jodie Kidd at £30k each.

Film director Michael Bay explains the source of actor Ben Affleck's expansive smile, 'We paid twenty thousand dollars for a set of pearly white teeth... he kinda had these baby teeth... so my dentist had Ben sitting in a dentist's chair for a week, eight hours a day.'

Creating a smile to enhance your charisma and dazzle your fans, though, is hardly just a case of a few fillings, a brace and lessons on dental hygiene. Numerous dental practitioners have become smile merchants offering a constantly enlarging armoury of techniques. Many are expensive and need repeating regularly. Today's smile merchants come from a long tradition of dedicated smile improvers.

Around the world, people have known for millennia that smiling can be a route to making a stronger impression. Ancient civilisations used materials resembling teeth for cosmetic replacements and restoration. Around 700BC, the Etruscans made dentures with ivory and bone. Early smile merchants even took teeth from the dead or purchased them from live donors. The results were usually terrible, yet the practice continued right up to the 1800s.

Teeth whitening and implants are a standard service of the smile industry. However, be cautious if you are contemplating these for boosting your confidence and charisma. In a survey of 350 dentists by the Chicago Dental Society, for example, four out of ten expressed concerns about their patients' excessively white smiles.

Implants too can trigger problems such as infections around the implant. Nerve damage can cause numbness, pain and ongoing tingling in the chin, lips or gums. The surgery can also potentially damage adjacent teeth or blood vessels.

Botox injections, sold to smile seekers as a way of reducing frowning and looking younger, are also no miracle cure. Physical problems can include making you look as if you have suffered a stroke, with eyelid droop, slurred speech, dropped mouth, asymmetrical forehead and even eyes that do not shut. Hardly helpful for your charisma!

More to the point, our ability to express emotion mainly depends on our facial expressions. If we have a few deep wrinkles, we probably own a highly expressive face. Research into leadership, for example, shows that people accurately assess others' levels of confidence, dominance, likeability and trustworthiness just by looking at facial expressions. If you Botox these out of existence it may undermine, not improve, your impact.

In all the talk about the 'Hollywood smile', 'smile makeovers' and even 'smile lifts', one fact remains: so much of charisma stems from what happens inside you that cosmetically tinkering with your smile may do little to enhance your impact – unless it also builds your confidence and self-esteem.

Smile power

The movie business and the need for stars to develop a strong charisma continue to direct an intense searchlight on the role of smiling.

Whole movie careers can spring from the strength of a smile. Julia Roberts, for example, routinely labelled as owning the 'most expensive smile in the world', only recently ceded this place to the star of *Ugly Betty*, who insured her awful smile for $10 million.

Ingrid Bergman famously made her first film appearance by popping out of a hotel room doorway, smiling, and asking for a morning paper. It immediately established her strong screen persona of the fresh-scrubbed, radiantly healthy, smiling extrovert.

If you are a woman trying to climb the real-life, slippery, corporate ladder, could plenty of smiling help you break through the so-called glass ceiling, or enhance your charisma?

Excessive smiling can potentially obstruct your charisma, since it fits our apparently unshakeable stereotype of what women are supposed to do. Social psychologist Nancy Henley graphically labels a woman's smile as 'her badge of appeasement', used to placate a more powerful male. The implication for women is that when interacting with powerful figures less is more. In social encounters for example, women smile 87 per cent of the time versus 67 per cent for men. Women are also 26 per cent more likely to return smiles from the opposite sex. Occasional smiling may prove better for your charisma than frequent smiles.

excessive smiling can potentially obstruct your charisma

If you tend to smile regardless of your emotional state, it will also not help your charisma. This is rootless smiling and women do plenty of it. It does not build charisma, and may even undermine it.

We have ways of making you smile

Jack Ma, founder of high-tech e-commerce company Alibaba.com, deliberately seeks smiling employees. 'When we hire people, we look for people who are naturally optimistic and happy...

it's hard to make a happy person unhappy, but it's even harder to make an unhappy person happy. I am able to tell whether a person is on our staff by their smile.'

This pressure to smile, to radiate happiness and even joy, is like an enforced kind of charisma. For example, countless jobs now demand that employees do more than just stand behind a counter or desk and answer questions. They must also offer ready smiles, whether they feel like it or not.

This demand for ready smiles stems from convincing evidence that the wider an employee's smile, the happier customers will be. Naturally, employers have taken note and acted accordingly. In US coffee shops, for example, researchers zealously watched 173 interactions between customers and employees. At various points during the transaction, they rated the strength of the employees' smile. The scale ranged from 'absent', to the maximum possible smile with exposed teeth. The researchers then asked the customers about their service experience. The bigger the employee's smile the more likely customers viewed that person as competent and felt the encounter to be satisfying. Customers also tended to leave larger tips for those servers who smiled than for ones who did not. This and other evidence continues to fuel the requirement for an enforced exhibition of smiling and a mandatory show of so-called charisma.

Compulsory smiling even infects the Olympics. For example, win or lose, synchronised swimmers not only co-ordinate their movements, they also all don identical nose clips and obligatory smiles. So too do Olympic acrobats, always ending their routine with a fixed and slightly apprehensive smile.

Will potential Chinese medal winners again receive coaching for the 2012 Olympics on the importance of smiling and be instructed to show between six and eight teeth? This happened in the previous Games even though it made them look as if they had swallowed a coat hanger.

Smile work out – 2

Do you know what makes you smile?

Here are 20 reasons someone gave during 2011:

Gerber daisies, lying in bed on a rainy morning, dancing, butterfly kisses, being with family, going home, getting Jeopardy! answers right, getting a good grade, reading Harry Potter, being in the sun, roller-skating, eating veggies, cooking, watching old musicals, children, swimming, singing songs I know the lyrics to, being with my closest friends, making others laugh, telling corny jokes.

Your turn

List five things that bring a smile to your face.

....

....

....

....

....

Use these as handy reminders when you feel short on smiling.

Why do these make you smile?

What is it about them that causes your reaction?

Does faking a smile help charisma?

Since smiling can enhance charisma it can seem sensible to keep on doing it, even if you have to pretend. However, fake smiles tend to be easily detected and therefore may do you more harm than good.

Famously, the nineteenth-century French physician Guillaume Duchenne identified two distinct types of smile, one of which you cannot fake. A Duchenne smile is the real one and involves contracting both the zygomatic major muscle – which raises the corners of the mouth – and the *orbicularis oculi* muscle – which raises the cheeks and forms crow's feet around the eyes.

You cannot directly control the second set of muscles. Even if you instruct your face to smile, your eyes will usually give you away. We learn from birth to detect these give-away signs of a false smile. People with genuine charisma literally smile with their eyes since they are using their inner smile to create a genuine external smile.

A non-Duchenne smile uses only the zygomatic major muscle. It was once known as the Pan-Am smile, because the flight attendants of the now defunct airline would flash every traveller the same, phoney grin. Now we call it the 'Botox smile', one that happens without the eyes taking part.

> *'Gordon Brown walked into his press conference wearing an alarming smile. It was wide and cavernous and was no doubt supposed to make him seem relaxed and assured. In fact, it looked as if aides had fixed him up with one of those clamps that dentists use to keep your mouth wide open. Then they had tugged it out and said: "Just hold it there for 20 seconds, prime minister!"*

> *Then the grimace collapsed and he resumed his normal apprehensive frown, like a nail-chewer who's realised that he's down to the cuticles and will soon be working on bloodied stumps.'*
>
> Simon Hoggart, *The Guardian*, 28 November 2007

Dacher Keltner, the psychology professor mentioned earlier, is an expert on the over 40 facial muscles used by humans to charm, smirk and appease. Commenting on real smiles, he mentions actor Julia Roberts, whose enormous smile is widely credited with making her into a super star.

'She has a wonderful smile, but it does not often reach her eyes in public,' he says. This is a kind way of saying she is faking it. If so, her career success may be due far more to her acting ability and other assets than her outsized grin.

'By contrast,' says Keltner, 'Angelina Jolie not only smiles broadly, and twinkles, but also tilts her head a little, which pushes the pleasurable body language into a higher gear. That is a smile which is impossible to resist.'

Chapter 12

Body language and eye contact

In our digitally driven world, with tweets, Facebook status updates, phone reminders and constant text messages, do body language and eye contact matter any more? With so much communication now online, increasingly shortened into a few terse sentences, it can seem rare for anyone to pay real attention to us. In fact, paying attention is almost a rare commodity.

Yet people still need to communicate face-to-face. With limited time to make a strong personal impact, you had better be good at it while you can. Body language and eye contact continue to contribute to charisma, so what will turn them to your advantage?

If you ever mastered riding a two-wheel bike, you will almost certainly recall it was mainly due to trial and error. Shouted instructions from an enthusiastic adult probably made no real difference.

Much the same applies to improving charisma using body language and eye contact. While there are plenty of handy lists for making these more effective, in practice they are like shouting at you with instructions. The main route to improvement remains the need to experiment with different approaches. Only that way will you discover whether they help or hinder your charisma.

Trial and error are relevant also because the precise balance between verbal and non-verbal behaviour for creating charisma remains in dispute. From advertising to popular psychology, for example, there are wild claims about the centrality of non-verbal behaviour in communication.

For example, the much-quoted but increasingly challenged communications model of Professor Albert Mehrabian implies words play only a minor part (7 per cent) in spoken communications, while facial movement and how words are actually spoken – tone of voice – count for the rest (93 per cent).

Others, like Howard Friedman, a psychology professor at the University of California, seem to confirm that through research experiments it is non-verbal cues, such as facial expression, gestures and body movements, that most affect and reveal the strength of someone's charisma. For example, charismatic leaders smile naturally, with wrinkling around the eyes, and touch people during conversations.

Yet such conclusions remain debatable. Do words truly count for so little, particularly in creating charisma? After all, some of the most charismatic individuals have been masters at framing language to ensnare their audiences. Lincoln, Churchill, Kennedy and Martin Luther King, for example, all created memorable sound bites that resonate down the ages, without their being physically present any more.

Churchill in particular was not especially attractive physically, nor did he have much sex appeal; however, his compelling personality came mainly through the power of his words. His 'blood, sweat and tears' speech, and admittedly haunting delivery, are widely credited with mobilising Great Britain to survive the Nazi assault.

what you say usually counts for much less than how you say it

Our main point here, though, is that what you say usually counts for much less than how you say it. That is, how you move and communicate in non-verbal ways will generally prove more persuasive in creating a memorable impact than just being highly articulate.

Body language

Our bodies 'talk' as eloquently as any uttered words. There is some truth in the claim made by some communications experts that the body cannot lie. It is almost impossible to eliminate or control tell-tale signs of what you are feeling and thinking. Unconscious movement, posture and gesture can all produce an effect and somtimes it is the opposite of one's intentions. Disconcertingly, even minor movements may have unpredictable results.

Consultants and personal coaches who work regularly with people on charisma enhancement often find their clients want specific help to control their body language or at least to understand it better. In particular, many fret unduly about what to do with their hands. Where should they put them, what gestures should they make, how can they use arms and hands more effectively?

Some who seek help even report having previously received 'rules', such as never make a gesture wider than your body, put your hands behind your back if you are unsure what to do with them, never sit down when presenting, and so on.

Rather than offering yet more rules, we usually start by inviting participants on our courses to talk on something they feel strongly about, something that really matters to them. Sure enough, within minutes we see them chatting happily, looking and sounding compelling, with no thought about what to do with their hands, eyes or their body. These simply take care of themselves.

What has changed from when they first started? Keen to communicate their concern, the person now devotes their entire attention to the audience, rather than themselves. This is the not-so 'secret' of mastering effective body language. When you stop being 'self-conscious' you can mainly leave your body to do the right thing.

Whatever the exact importance of body language, it can certainly affect charisma. For example, if your body language fails to match your spoken words, you are wasting your time trying to make an impact. Equally, using a normally positive body gesture, such as nodding or leaning forward, at the wrong time can undermine the impression you make.

Charisma killers

- Interrupting when people tell their stories.
- When listening, showing you disagree strongly by shaking your head or using sarcasm.
- Leaning back expansively with your arms behind your head.
- Doodling, using a laptop, fiddling with your mobile while others are talking or presenting.
- Folding your arms across your chest.
- Slouching in a chair, with one leg over the arm.
- Yawning while talking or listening.
- Picking at fingernails, lips or at imaginary lint on your clothes.
- Tapping fingers impatiently on a table or chair.
- Staring glassy-eyed without blinking at someone.
- Invading someone's personal space without their invitation – 'acceptable' space can vary considerably across national cultures.
- Biting your nails.
- Chewing on a pencil or pen when talking to someone.
- Wiping your palms on your clothing – instead use a handkerchief or tissue.

Posture

There is an enjoyable moment in the first Christopher Reeves' *Superman* film when he stops being mild-mannered Clark Kent and morphs into Superman. Without the help of digital techniques, Reeves visibly 'grows' taller. He does it by removing his glasses, raising his head upright, standing fully erect, pushing out his chest and thrusting his admittedly bulky shoulders well back.

Posture says a lot about you. An erect posture makes you look confident and self-assured. For example, apart from standing straight and making sure your shoulders do not sag, imagine an invisible string from the ceiling pulling the top of your head upwards.

an erect posture makes you look confident and self-assured

To 'programme' your body to be more erect, try walking around at home for ten minutes balancing a book on your head. Do this daily for a week, and you will soon feel the difference between your current normal posture and being truly, proudly erect. This classic, yet still relevant, posture exercise may initially feel awkward, stiff and even pompous or arrogant, but it will gradually straighten you up and come to feel natural.

The alternative of slouching may seem comfortable, but visually it suggests to others that you are down on yourself and not in a good place mentally.

Leaning is almost a whole language of its own. For example, propping yourself against walls or tables can suggest you are tired or lazy. Leaning forward in your seat usually indicates you are giving careful attention to the other person.

Tilting back in your chair to rest on two legs is one of those gestures that may send conflicting messages. While it can suggest confidence, equally it may reveal a lack of respect for your audience. Worse, you also run the risk of looking silly when you accidentally fall backwards.

If you become fully engaged with your audience, you will be less likely to adopt unconscious distracting body gestures, such as shuffling, drawing patterns with your feet on the floor, or walking in small circles. In one-to-one conversations, if you focus entirely on the other person you will be less likely to turn away in mid-sentence or show disinterest in continuing the conversation.

Translating body language

- Tilt your head to one side during a conversation while looking at the other person intensely. *'I'm interested in what you are saying and thinking about it.'*
- Take deep, short breaths. *'I'm nervous right now.'*
- Nod and smile as the person speaks. *'As you can see, I am paying attention.'*
- Walk with even strides and avoid running. Look ahead or in front of you, not at the floor. *'I am calm and self-assured.'*
- Arms closed around you, even shoved into pockets. *'I'm not really interested in what you're saying and feel defensive.'*
- Body gesture is open, with face-up palms. *'I am an honest and straightforward person.'*
- Stroking your chin slowly, and deliberately. *'I am considering a decision and thinking about the choices.'*
- Making a steeple out of your hands and looking focused. *'I'm receptive to what you say and am sure of myself.'*
- Smiling, but only if it is genuine and comes from the heart. *'I like you and what you are saying.'*
- Removing tie and jacket and opening shirt top collar button. *'I'm comfortable with these surroundings.'*
- Rolling up your sleeves or down according to the situation. *'Let's get down to work.'*
- Clenching fists. *'I'm feeling angry, probably at you, watch out!'*

- Rubbing or wringing your hands together. 'I simply don't know what to do.' 'I feel very unsure of myself.'
- Scratching your head. 'I am puzzled and uncertain.'
- When asked for an honest answer, stroking your nose, playing with your hair, rubbing your eyes, constantly touching your nose. 'I am probably lying or less than honest.'
- Tapping your fingers on a table or arms of a chair. 'This is making me anxious.'

Warning: A single body gesture is seldom enough to accurately convey these messages. They usually need to be a part of a more holistic approach that includes other aspects of behaviour that support the message.

Hands

John F. Kennedy regarded personal style as so important that before running for president he reportedly commissioned a study to determine the most effective handshake.

As Kennedy knew, the act of touching another human being can instantly collect and send a huge amount of information. Designed for precisely that purpose, your handshake can play an important role in initially strengthening or undermining your charisma, as other people experience it.

For example, according to some interpersonal experts, the strength of your handshake potentially conveys one of three simple messages: This person is trying to dominate me; I can dominate this person; and I feel comfortable with this person. Similarly, the 'dead fish' handshake, regrettably often given by women, can be destructive by conveying low self-esteem and a lack of personal self-belief.

Both the extremes of bone-crushing handshakes and limp ones can dent your charisma. If you happen to possess one of these you may be unaware of it. As with bad breath, to get at the truth it may be sensible to ask a trusted friend for some personal feedback.

Studies also suggest that a dominant person turns their palm down during a handshake, while the more submissive person shakes with the palm facing up. Aim for a straight up and down, firm handshake.

Charisma courtesy

Watch those with genuine charisma and how the combination of many small movements or gestures often makes a disproportionate impact on those around them. Being extremely courteous, for instance, can leave a strong, positive impression in the minds of those on the receiving end. For example:

- Open doors and allow others to walk before you. Only excessively narcissistic charisma seekers barge ahead as if they own the planet.
- Cough or sneeze into a tissue or handkerchief, not the face of those around you. (Both, though, are deadly in Japan.)
- Shake hands briefly, not for a prolonged time, unless you know the person well.
- You may feel genuinely affectionate if you ruffle someone's hair in a formal setting, but it suggests you are being condescending.
- Talk on the phone in a calm, volume-controlled voice – avoid shouting.
- In a crowd of people, get out and mingle rather than huddling in a corner with your mobile phone; keep your private conversations for when you're alone.
- In the middle of a discussion, refuse to take a phone call.
- No matter how angry you are, shut doors quietly, don't slam them.

(See also Chapter 9, Demeanour.)

Preparing the body

Generating charisma requires energy and you may need to wake up your body when you really want to make an impression on people. Before an important performance, actors spend an hour or more preparing their bodies. They work hard to unwind, relax and get themselves ready to communicate. You can usefully do this too, whenever you intend to achieve a significant impact on people.

Effective physical relaxation exercises include shaking separate parts of your body to remove tension; closing eyes and focusing on each part of the body in turn checking for tension; breathing in deeply and out slowly, while telling that part to let go and relax.

Similarly, use voice exercises to loosen the throat and vocal cords. For example, to help loosen your speech muscles, in private hum gently, make simple sounds such as aahhs and oos; say a tongue twister aloud, such as 'Red Leather, Yellow Leather, Red Leather, Yellow Leather'.

Physical exercise warms up and enlivens your mind, body, breath and voice, so you are ready to fully use your charisma.

Eye contact

Eye contact, smiling and other non-verbal behaviour combine to create your charisma. Like smiling, eye contact proves a highly efficient method of connecting with people, building rapport, creating personal chemistry and therefore affecting charisma. It is an easy way of sending the message: 'I want to interact with you.'

Other benefits include reducing tension in conversation, conveying an image of assertiveness and showing respect. While the eyes may be the 'windows of the soul' it is mainly the various muscles that surround them that ultimately do the communicating. (See Chapter 11 on Smiling.)

In some cultures eye contact might be used to say what cannot be said directly. For instance, someone working for an Asian company might ask, 'Are you happy with my work' and receive the answer, 'Oh yes, perfectly happy.' But the reply might be given with a sad look that contradicts the actual words. Miss the look and you miss the real message.

Improving your charisma may require you to give more attention than you currently do to eye contact. See the Health check below.

Eye contact health check

	For each question decide whether you:	AGREE	DISAGREE
1	When I am with people I seldom hold eye contact for long		
2	At work, there is no need to give much eye contact		
3	It's embarrassing when senior people give me eye contact		
4	When talking to someone I naturally scan the rest of the room for what's happening		
5	I find it awkward when someone I don't know gives me eye contact		
6	Eye contact worries me, you never know where it might lead		
7	I need to make a special effort to give eye contact to those around me ***If you agree with any of these seven statements, it suggests you may not be currently making the best of your charisma.***		

While the act of making eye contact is familiar, the actual process consists of various distinct stages. Each may have a specific kind of impact on people at the time and also dissolve seamlessly into the next one.

- Contact
- Maintain
- Break off
- Return and renew.

Contact

This is the brief moment when eyes meet – perhaps across a crowded room or maybe close up.

Usually it occurs without conscious effort. People with a strong charisma will often convert it into a defining moment, one which those on the receiving end may ever afterwards recall. The experience can prove so compelling that, when talking about it later, they make it seem mystical, or personally transforming.

What exactly creates this magical moment?

It stems partly from the sheer concentration and focus the person with charisma devotes to the particular moment. Extreme charismatics invest it with an intensity and intimacy that raises it above the ordinary. Their direct gaze makes you feel as if together you are the only two people in the room.

So powerful is this initial contact that sometimes people on the receiving end seem mesmerised. As one Bill Clinton watcher observed, 'It's not that Clinton seduces women. It's that he seduces everyone.'

The unmistakeable initial message someone with Extreme Charisma seems to be sending is along the lines of: 'I see you, I know who you are, and I want to connect with you.' In some cases, the unspoken message is perhaps far simpler; it is: 'I love you.'

When you have an extremely strong intent (Aim) it drives your gaze and your eye contact starts to become incredibly powerful. It's as if your eyes are talking directly to the other person, but without speaking the actual words. (See Chapter 2, Aim.)

Sometimes the initial contact with eyes is linked to a physical gesture involving touch, such as a handshake, a pat on the shoulder, an additional grasp of the arm. These can add an extra, disarming intimacy to a first encounter.

Maintain

Influential people excel at maintaining eye contact. They will hold it for a considerable time, often combining it with a subtle use of personal space. For example, getting physically closer to the person they have in their sights, yet not so close that it seems threatening, rather than friendly.

when maintaining eye contact, charismatics devote their entire attention to it

When maintaining eye contact, charismatics devote their entire attention to it; they do not permit anything to distract them. They robustly resist interruptions such as the temptation to look over the person's shoulder or to scan the surroundings for something more interesting.

During this important stage of eye contact, the positive but unspoken messages being sent are often basic yet unmistakeable. They include:

'I like you.'

'Right now I want to be with you and no one else.'

'I am really interested in you.'

'You are interesting.'

'What you're saying matters.'

'I'm listening to you with my full attention.'

'You really matter to me.'

'I agree with you.'

'Tell me more.'

Although prolonged eye contact is part of creating charisma, be wary of formal rules such as 'hold contact for at least 45 seconds'.

Excessive eye contact can be as counter-productive as too little. A solid, unblinking gaze at someone can be disconcerting and even threatening. Avoid an uncomfortable stare and instead drop your eyes briefly towards something else, such as a document, to jot down a note, to admire someone's hair, dress or appearance.

Be aware of an important cultural dimension in respect of eye contact. While Westerners generally regard prolonged eye contact as attractive, it may be seen as disrespectful in certain Asian environments.

Break off

Those with a strong charisma turn the ending of eye contact into a deliberate part of saying goodbye. That is, they do not make the mistake of breaking eye contact for no apparent reason.

They imbue the ending with verbal and non-verbal signs of regret that they must move on. The ending becomes a significant event not a casual one. For example, they may give an extra smile, or nod to indicate an ending and it's time to close the contact. Or they may give a subtle, brief look away to signal an ending is coming.

Having established good eye contact, you will weaken your Charisma Effect if you abruptly drop your gaze without reason.

Return and renew

This is said to be the secret of extreme charismatics such as Bill Clinton and Steve Jobs. It has acquired its own pseudo-scientific term of Reality Distortion Field.

It works like this. Having moments ago ended eye contact and moved on, the charismatic person deliberately looks back at the other person and seals the deal with a short, renewed eye contact.

Along with other non-verbal cues, this renewal of eye contact sends attractive, unspoken messages such as 'I enjoyed talking to you', 'I am already missing you', 'Hope to see you again', 'I will be back in touch', 'Don't forget me'.

It takes practice to do Return and renew, not least because you have to remember to actually do it when you are already beginning to focus on someone else.

Eye contact work out

1 During every day this week, practise making brief eye contact with strangers. Look at the eyes of every person walking towards you and note their eye colour. Take less than a second, then look away. No one minds, and you will soon be comfortable with the whole process.
2 Practise longer contact with waiters, sales clerks and other service staff. Keep a neutral facial expression. Practise this for at least a week.
3 When talking with someone in a room with other people, practise focusing entirely on one person for long enough to make them smile and give you similar attention. Don't worry if they do not do it well, or look over your shoulder at other people.
4 Having made good eye contact with someone, practise leaning back and lowering your voice. See what effect it has on the other person.
5 During prolonged eye contact with someone, stand slightly sideways to them and without facing them, and make an opportunity to pat or touch them on the back, arm, shoulder.

6 While talking to someone and giving eye contact, mentally keep saying the following: 'I am really interested in what you have to say. You are a fascinating person I could talk to all day.' Notice how this mental process begins to affect not only how you give eye contact but the rest of your body language.

7 In conversation with someone, practise noticing whenever your mind starts drifting – to a nearby discussion, to getting the train home, to something that occurred in the office today, and so on.

Focus your inner attention on the person you are talking to and whenever it drifts bring it back to the one you are talking to at the moment.

Making it real

When it comes to body language and eye contact, if charismatics have a secret, it is making their words match their gestures.

You can do all the right things as far as body language and eye contact are concerned and still get it spectacularly wrong. It is only when the timing of your non-verbal communication works in combination with your words that the total effect becomes impressive. Since charisma comes from within, this means allowing your feelings to steer your body movements and not the other way around. Trust your feelings and you can trust your body language.

trust your feelings and you can trust your body language

Start paying attention to the dynamics of the movement of people whose presence you admire. When they gesture, is it smooth or does it explode? Does it start off slowly, increasing momentum until it ends abruptly? Or does it do the opposite, starting off fast only to fizzle out in the end? What are they saying in connection with the movement?

When your body is in sync with your words you feel more con fident and the impact becomes so much greater. By taking charge of the communication flow through your body movements and words you will be able to persuade others more easily, and to take charge of many of the human interactions that occur throughout the day.

Chapter 13

Leadership and charisma

Are you a charismatic leader? If not, does it matter and what can you do about it? Because of the popular view that leaders must be charismatic, many executives, particularly those running big corporations, now reach for personal coaching and mentoring to help strengthen their flagging charisma.

If you can inspire others and convey a strong vision of the future, you may have what it takes to be a chief executive. For you, 'CEO' perhaps stands for Charismatic, Energetic and Outgoing. Leaders like this include Richard Branson, Philip Green (who runs the enormously profitable Arcadia Group) and Stuart Rose of Marks & Spencer.

for you, 'CEO' perhaps stands for Charismatic, Energetic and Outgoing

The charisma of Larry Ellison, who founded Oracle Corporation in 1977 and was still there over 30 years later, is equally well established. Widely known beyond his own industry, Larry's compelling charisma was once summed up by one of his executives as: 'The difference between God and Larry Ellison is that God does not believe that he is Larry.'

Charismatic leaders may make a big impression but equally can be entirely ego-driven, narcissistic and achieve results mainly at the expense of others. Robert Maxwell was a notorious example of misplaced leadership charisma. A bully with flashes of charm, he tried to intimidate and dominate all those he encountered, caring little about the price others paid for his high profile.

There is also ample evidence from research that it is possible to be a successful leader without possessing a large dose of charisma. Despite this, the general expectation remains that leaders should manifest exceptional charisma. For example, when choosing new chief executives, selection boards generally gravitate towards those candidates with a forceful charisma, rather than with a record of actual achievement.

However, anyone who thinks it is worth paying extra for a CEO with charisma should think again. The better a company's performance, the more its stakeholders conclude that its boss has charisma. Consequently a 2006 study warned that boards of directors 'need to be cautious when considering the potential benefits of charismatic leaders.' This same report concluded that CEO charisma bears 'little or no relationship to a company's future performance.'

Jim Collins' seminal study *Good to Great* made a convincing case against seeking charismatic leadership. He similarly found that those leading the most successful companies were models of duality – modest and wilful, humble and fearless. They never wanted to become larger-than-life heroes, nor did they aspire to being on a pedestal. 'They were seemingly ordinary people quietly producing extraordinary results. They were more like Socrates and Lincoln than Patton or Caesar.'

Speaking from personal experience, the late Dame Anita Roddick, founder of the Body Shop, likewise asserted, 'You don't necessarily have to be charismatic. You just have to believe in what you are doing so strongly that it becomes a reality.'

Charisma persistence

Originally coined by the nineteenth-century sociologist Max Weber to describe inspirational leadership, charisma continues to play a key role today in how people view leaders. There is however some logic in this. Like it or not, we are driven by basic urges rooted in our need to survive. Quite simply, we look for the strongest, most powerful person to save us from tigers.

In most Western countries, you cannot expect to succeed in politics without a fair slice of charisma to show you inspire devotion and are a change agent. Richard Nixon famously lost the charisma battle with Kennedy not only because of how he looked; he was also humourless, told no jokes, had no amusing stories, said or did nothing that conveyed affection of any kind. His charisma was almost non-existent, but sheer doggedness eventually helped him overcome this limitation. Likewise, the subsequent two Bush presidents were similarly charisma-challenged, having little mass appeal. Whatever explains their success, it was almost certainly not due to the force of their personalities.

So, given the persistent link between charisma and leadership, what does it mean to be a charismatic leader? US leadership guru Warren Bennis concluded, 'Charisma is the result of effective leadership and not the other way around.' The implication is that to be an effective leader first do the job well, and let your charisma take care of itself.

Multiple studies show charismatic leaders possessing a presence: a presence of mind, a quality of the eyes, physical beauty, confidence, endurance, unusual mental attainment and the power to evoke an emotional response from an audience. The full list goes on seemingly forever. Even if you could somehow acquire all of the qualities identified, you would still not necessarily be seen as a leader, let alone a charismatic one.

According to Howard Friedman, a psychology professor at the University of California who claims to be able to measure charisma, it comes down to non-verbal cues such as facial expression, gestures and body movements. For example, charismatic leaders smile naturally, with wrinkling around the eyes, and touch people during conversations. (See also Chapter 12.)

Absolute essentials

The long list of attributes, traits and qualities identified by researchers and others makes the search for what will create leadership charisma into a will o' the wisp. The only viable route to building your charismatic leadership is through specific, observable behaviours. Based on the present body of knowledge, to be a charismatic leader you need to:

- Show passion, energy and confidence to gain people's attention
- Bring vision and goals to life
- Use your personality and ideas to build relationships
- Employ outstanding persuasion and negotiating skills
- Take responsibility.

All of these are learnable and susceptible to improvement through practice.

Passion, energy and confidence

Charismatic leaders use their obvious passion or commitment to gain people's attention and infiltrate their hearts and minds. Singapore's founder, Lee Kuan Yew, for example, combined a compelling mix of logic, emotion and passion to make his leadership acceptable and even attractive, even while still exercising tight control over both followers and non-followers.

In contrast, Hosni Mubarak of Egypt, ex head of RBS Fred Goodwin, and Jeff Skilling of Enron all used their passion inappropriately and for selfish ends. There is a fine line between demagoguery and a passion in which enthusiasm and commitment carries both you and others away.

In over two decades of developing corporate leaders at Maynard Leigh, we have seldom encountered a successful leader with excess passion. Few suffer from so much enthusiasm that they overwhelm and antagonise others. Instead, we are far more likely to encounter an absence of passion.

Many at the top of organisations, particularly large ones, seem prone to declining enthusiasm and joy for what they are doing. Putting it slightly differently, work eventually rather loses its meaning.

However, the good news is that we do not easily lose our passion. Even when grown rusty, it will still be there. When you re-light the fuse, eyes start to sparkle, bodies straighten, attention to surroundings rises, and relationship to others increases.

So how would you describe your passion? Is it brimming over? Do you hunger to tell others how you feel about your goals? Do you itch to share your vision, and how it might be realised?

Passion work out

1. List what inspires you – makes you feel excited, energised and alive – persist at this, take your time arriving at an answer.
2. Identify on your list what really matters in your present leadership role.
3. Now describe your passion using a metaphor, a story or an analogy – bring it to life so that someone you have just met 'gets it' right away.
4. Next, find three other people outside your immediate sphere of influence and ask them what inspires them and why. How do these people look and sound when they talk about it?
5. Try summing up your passion in a single short paragraph and video yourself explaining it. What do you see? Do you look and sound enthusiastic? How authentic is that person you are watching?
6. This week, invite those who report direct to you to talk about *their* vision – what inspires them. How does it compare with yours?
7. For the next month do one thing every day that communicates your leadership passion to people, without turning it into a lecture or something they have to do.

People will be more likely to see you as a charismatic leader if through your passion you also demonstrate abundant personal energy. Some experts consider the energy factor the single biggest reason for choosing a leader. 'Never, ever, ever, ever, ever, promote a human being to any position who does not vibrate, who does not give off intensity, who does not literally exude energy', is how renowned consultant and writer Tom Peters puts it.

Like every human being, you consist of energy and certainly possess it. However, only when you transform this into actual behaviour can you expect to affect others. Highly energetic people – often regarded as charismatic – can fill a room with a joyous, mesmerising and inspiring presence. The management and focus of personal energy plays an important part in whether you create a lasting and memorable impression.

Actors know all about energy management and are a good source of help en route to charismatic leadership. They learn to express energy through their bodies, voice, language, and use of space and time. There are useful acting techniques you can adopt to build your charisma without turning you into an actor. For example, you might explore what is *not* said, reading body language and using personality types.

Confidence

Few genuine leaders lack confidence; yet this may still be a concern if inside you feel differently from how you actually behave. This may happen if you are someone who continually wants 'the right answers', or if you are technically excellent yet find it uncomfortable dealing with ambiguity, which pervades the leadership task.

It is one of the many paradoxes of leadership that people on the receiving end of your charisma need to experience both your vulnerability and your confidence. By exposing aspects of your vulnerability, you reveal your approachability and humanity. This makes you more 'human' and builds rather than undermines your leadership charisma. Alongside that, when you exude confidence you encourage people to put their trust in you. No wonder that one of the most startling questions to pose to managers who aspire to lead is: 'Why should anyone be led by you?'

people on the receiving end of your charisma need to experience both your vulnerability and your confidence

How real does your confidence have to be? Can you fake it? Obviously many leaders do manage to demonstrate impressive confidence, while inside they are quivering wrecks of uncertainty and nerves. But this is doing it the hard way. Keeping up a constant façade of confidence is extremely stressful and those who do it often fool themselves that people do not see through the charade.

This is why your willingness to share your vulnerability becomes so critical. Being ready to admit, for example, that 'I don't know' is far more powerful in establishing your credibility and building your charisma than trying to cling to the illusion that you are sure of everything you do as a leader.

So how do you acquire and, through your charisma, exude the kind of leadership confidence that makes people want to follow you? Apart from showing your vulnerability and human side, start with your gut instinct and do what you think is right. This means accepting that on occasions you are going to fail – all humans do.

Confident leaders also avoid the enervating experience of decisional regret. This well-known phenomenon undermines both the actual decision process and leadership itself. When you make a decision, commit and go for it. Don't continually second guess yourself. If you have to change course, you have to change course. If you never commit, all you will ever do is change course.

if you never commit, all you will ever do is change course

Confidence is also shown by your readiness to have fun and enjoy leading. Why expect your direct reports to demonstrate positive enthusiasm if they do not see passion and energy coming from you? Confidence also comes across when you reveal more courage than fear. If direct reports read worry and concern on your face they will begin to lose confidence in your ability to show them the way forward.

You may not be able to instantly don a coat of convincing leadership confidence, as this usually arrives from experience and trial and error, but you can give your natural confidence a flying start if you are willing to look inside yourself to explore what is happening when you have negative feelings that potentially undermine your leadership impact. For example, try exploring the different personality types inside you that can radically affect your ability to exude confidence.

Personality types

An effective approach drawn from the world of acting is learning to tap into different personality types inside you. Actors know from experiences what recent brain scan research now confirms. Within the brain, separate selves quite clearly exist as sub-personalities and some can even be located in specific parts of the left and right hemispheres.

For example, inside you might be a child, parent, teacher, bully, joker, lazybones, adventurer, poet, worrier, carer, hero, coward, lover, sage, salesperson and so on. These personalities can affect how you interact with people and ultimately your charisma. Charismatic leaders tap into them to direct and influence how they come across to people.

Personality type work out

1. Set aside half an hour for this work out. Sit quietly alone. Have a pad and pen nearby.
2. Think about some of the most familiar characters or 'personalities' inside you. Identify at least six. Allow yourself plenty of time to arrive at your chosen ones.
3. Write down who they are. For example, air traffic controller, couch potato, wimp, efficiency expert, Mrs Nosey, Action hero.
4. In your mind, say 'hello' to each character. Introduce each in turn to an imaginary audience and ask each to describe what they do. If possible, do this aloud, allowing yourself to inhabit or embody this character. That is, briefly you 'become' this person.
5. Now consider each of these characters in turn. Which serve your charisma well and which don't, and why?
6. 'Thank' the positive ones for their help and invite them to describe how they might help next time you want to make an impact with people.
7. Say 'goodbye' to the less positive ones and ask them to stay in the background and only appear when you specifically call them up.

Bring vision and goals alive

The CEO of the Indian company HCL Technologies, Vineet Nayar, first presented himself to its 26,000 employees by famously dancing in the isles of numerous theatres around the world, each filled with several thousand staff. His outrageous action both captured their attention and drove home his two initial messages: that he valued informality, and that he was a human being with real failings – he manifestly could not dance too well!

Charismatic leaders like Nayar do not merely talk about what they want to achieve; they develop a knack of making their aim seem within reach, no matter how far away it appears right now.

One way they do this is by concretising their vision, using multiple ways of making the vision come alive for the listeners.

At HCL Nayar later promulgated his wider mission for the company as 'Employees first, customers second.' This back-to-front message says that satisfied employees leads to satisfied customers and is also adopted by entrepreneur Richard Branson in running the Virgin empire. It drives consultants in customer care, shareholders and other traditionalists crazy. Yet by concretising the aim, Nayar and Branson bring the vision alive for everyone.

Concretising is how a vision or goal acquires a degree of seeming inevitability. That well-known clichéd introduction of a political hopeful as 'the next president of the United States' is just one well-worn example of trying to make the vision seem almost within reach.

Studies of US presidents now labelled by historians as charismatic found they were heavy users of image-based words. The most effective ones adopted more image-evoking words in pivotal speeches.

You can help people by offering tangible examples that bring the vision into sharp focus. One way is by demonstrating it through your own behaviour. This may seem entirely obvious, yet leaders often lose sight of the importance of showing the way, of being a role model for their vision.

Expect also to tailor how you describe the vision to fit the audience and use a variety of communication vehicles. Apple's Steve Jobs brings his vision alive in the minds of his devoted audience through combining fantastic technical insight with his ability to understand the market.

While the above describes a process that charismatic leaders use, you will need to work on discovering what it is about you and your vision that is compelling. As one leadership expert puts it: 'You can't borrow someone else's charisma.'

Build relationships

If there is a single golden thread running through creating leadership charisma, it is your ability to relate to others. Being charismatic does not mean you build a relationship with everyone who crosses your path. It is not about endless connections. Who you connect with depends on what your aim is (see Chapter 2).

Charismatic leaders develop advanced interpersonal relationship skills, particularly emotional intelligence. That is, they become experts at relating to people, for example through rapport, to gain the attention they need to persuade and influence.

The interpersonal relationship skills of charismatic leaders include the ability to communicate with passion, use body language, tell captivating stories, show empathy and tap into mood.

Relationship work out

1. Choose a day in which you will consciously listen to others and be curious about what motivates them.
2. Make time to hear from those who disagree with you – one CEO used to refuse to make a decision if everyone around the table agreed on it. He insisted on more time for 'disagreements to surface.'
3. Create multiple opportunities for divergent views to emerge.
4. How will you demonstrate that as a leader you care about what others think?
5. Pay attention to the extent to which you smile and seek eye contact with people.
6. Master re-framing, so you can convey your ideas in different ways to meet people's needs.

Employ outstanding persuasion skills

Aristotle wrote about persuasion techniques 2,000 years ago, and the methods have been growing ever since. Charismatic leaders are great at selling themselves and their ideas. Within organisations, charismatic leaders are often experts in their area of influence. First, they are good at demonstrating where things are going wrong, for example the inadequacy of existing technology or the failure of the current status quo to deliver results or achieve the shared vision.

charismatic leaders are great at selling themselves and their ideas

Secondly, they are good at challenging the existing order through using unconventional means. This may take the form of an entrepreneurial style, but equally it can stem from using insight and imagination to offer unusual strategies. For example, James Dyson's perception that air fans did not need rotating blades seemed counter intuitive, until he produced one without blades that was more efficient than current models.

Seven ways in which charismatic leaders persuade and influence

1 Build trust – give people a credible reason to follow your lead. Work on becoming the kind of person people rely on and see as an expert, or wise person.

2 Use appropriate body language and voice – these can demonstrate why people should trust and respect you. (See Chapter 12.)

3 Show confidence – people want self-assured leaders. They are waiting for you to step up and lead. Right or wrong, confidence can be more important to others than competence, whether they realise it or not.

4 Be highly articulate – this includes being able to explain the context in which you want to achieve your vision or goal, and clarifying your own

motivation – 'why this matters to me.' It also involves using attractive language – hone your ability to paint compelling word pictures, tell engaging stories, create vibrant metaphors and analogies that engage your audience.

5 Take centre stage – be willing to step into the limelight to make your case, often in the face of resistance or scepticism (see below).
6 Take responsibility – see below.
7 Use unconventional behaviour – charismatic leaders often persuade through their innovative behaviour that may run counter to existing norms.

Take centre stage

In the film *The Devil Wears Prada* there is a defining moment when the powerful fashion editor sits quietly in her limousine while outside the curious crowd jostles to peer inside. She tells her acolyte that naturally 'Everyone wants to be us'. Meanwhile, her acolyte is thinking entirely differently. Sometimes charismatic leaders cannot even conceive of a world in which they are not the centre of attention.

Leaders who make a lasting impact do several things to stand up for what they believe.

First, like the fashion editor, they come to expect the limelight. They take for granted that people want to meet or hear them and act accordingly. For example, watch a successful leader arrive at a reception desk for a meeting. Even though directed to a seat to await the call, a genuine leader will often stand impatiently by the desk, conveying the clear message: 'I am important and expect to receive attention soon.'

Act as if you expect to command an audience. Rather than 'I wonder if people will pay attention to what I have to say', show by your positive demeanour that naturally people will want to hear your message, and indeed have little choice. Do this from a position of quiet confidence, rather than being arrogant and insensitive to others in your urge to pass on your message.

Secondly, leaders whose charisma makes a lasting impression are courageous. They are willing to go against the grain, stir things up and express a contrary opinion to others. This is charisma in action, a readiness to be different, to stand out from the crowd, even in some cases to be opinionated.

Thirdly, even when a successful leader is deep down retiring and self-effacing, nothing stops them from explaining their vision and sharing what they want to achieve.

Centre stage work out

1. Act as if people are keen to hear what you have to say.
2. Be ready to take a contrary view and stick with it in the face of opposition.
3. 'Demand' your rightful air time in meetings and other gatherings, without always waiting to be asked to speak.
4. Approach each new situation and encounter by asking yourself: 'How can I make a difference here?'
5. Once you have people's attention, use humour and powerful stories to keep their interest.
6. Refine your core message until it is so familiar it becomes part of who you are.

Take responsibility

Louis Gerstner was a charismatic leader. He was a non-technocrat who in the early 1990s took on the challenge of transforming IBM, an ultra-technological company that was apparently in terminal decline. His particular charisma reflected a combination of drive, motivation, integrity, self-confidence, intelligence, business knowledge and emotional intelligence. Other key competencies included tenacity, openness, assertiveness and trustworthiness.

Most notably he took responsibility. First, he was passionate about execution, getting things done, not crafting strategy but implementing it. Secondly, he took the lead in creating a high-performance culture that set goals, measured results and ensured accountability.

Charismatic leaders will usually be reformers who, like Gerstner, step forward to make things happen. They say things like: 'I'll do that', 'leave that to me', 'I'll sort it out', 'my solution to that is…', 'there must be a better way'.

They also acquire a reputation for standing their ground. This means when things go awry or something needs sorting they do not run and hide; instead, they will speak up when something is wrong and offer to sort it out.

Taking responsibility also means they are willing to make tough decisions and defend them vigorously.

Another aspect of taking responsibility is readiness to hear uncomfortable or bad news without attributing blame to those who draw attention to it. This encourages people to come forward and share what is happening. Richard Branson, for example, is known for his ever-ready notebook in which he notes down information from staff and customers. With more than 35,000 employees, he receives over 50 emails a day from non-managerial staff drawing attention to issues that require attention. He addresses each concern by either answering personally or initiating some action.

Faking it

Misguided, impatient or desperate leaders sometimes ask, 'Can't I just fake charisma?' Some personal coaches, perhaps struggling to help severely charisma-challenged clients, claim you can fake charisma. Their approach relies on two simple principles:

1. Drawing on past emotions to drive your desired outward behaviour.
2. Adopting assertive body postures that create hormonal shifts which in turn affect your real emotions and how others perceive you.

Past emotions

Actors learn to tap into their past emotions to recreate the effects, on demand. In particular, method acting requires the actor to identify relevant past emotional experiences then 'relive' these until they feel entirely real. Leaders too can adopt this approach. For a while it may help you exude confidence and through it create at least the appearance of charisma.

For example, you think of a real event in the past when you felt excited, assured and energised. You practise 'reliving' that experience, until it becomes so real again that you carry it with you into your contact with people. Because you are reliving a 'real' emotion, you are more likely to appear convincing than if you mechanically tried to behave that way. This approach, though, requires plenty of practice.

Positive postures

Alternatively, you can deliberately put your body into positive, assertive positions that convey confidence, power and energy. For example, shoulders back, an erect stance, head held high, standing with your hands on your hips and so on. Strangely, just placing your body in such positive positions supposedly triggers changes in your brain – for instance, causing hormonal shifts linked to power and dominance or feelings of certainty.

If your body acts like you are confident and powerful this stimulates you to start feeling that way too. Since feelings have a greater effect on people than what you say, 'forced' body posture can help you come across more strongly than perhaps you feel inside.

Acting 'as if' you are confident, energised, interested, charismatic by making your body do those things that convey these messages is quick and relatively easy. To some extent it is more a way of fooling yourself into behaving in ways that seem convincing. If you can convince yourself through your physical posture that you are charismatic, then that is how you may come across.

As with forced smiling, though, people you encounter have a powerful, inbuilt ability to detect fakery and bullshit. They often do it without even understanding how they do it. They just *know* the real thing when they see it. Faking charismatic behaviour is technically possible, though leaders who rely on this tend to be quickly unmasked, undermining rather than building their impact.

Doing without charisma

'I'm not into the personality stuff', claimed Bart Becht, the man behind Mr Sheen polish, Clearasil spot cream and Cillit Bang® limescale remover. 'A high profile normally goes with taking the credit and that would send the wrong messages... this isn't a one-man show.'

Becht, a notorious workaholic, and rarely interviewed when head of global company Reckitt Benckiser Group Plc, finally stepped down as Chief Executive Officer in 2011. He had spent more than a decade at the helm of the household-cleanser company he had formed, yet he hardly rated on the charisma scale in terms of public profile.

Business leaders like Becht, Marjorie Scardino (head of Pearson Group which publishes this book), and Richard Cousins (chief executive officer of the world's largest foodservice company, the Compass Group) fly beneath the celebrity radar yet consistently produce excellent commercial results.

Not every society or every organisation wants or even needs charismatic leaders. Some have every reason to avoid such characters, having experienced them as bullies, ego-maniacs, and sometimes inhuman despots.

A charisma-free successful leader might seem a contradiction in terms, yet some do manage to succeed. Examples include Prime Minister Manmohan Singh of India, French President Nicolas Sarkozy, former British Prime Minister Tony Blair, German Chancellor Angela Merkel, and Alan Greenspan, former chairman of the Federal Reserve who won legions of followers by the depth of his thinking.

Perhaps then it is time to stop bothering about charisma altogether? On balance, though, most successful leaders do manage to wind up their charisma so they make a memorable impression.

Leadership without charisma

- Rely on deeds not words
- Make things happen
- Do not worry about looks
- Be more concerned with doing the right thing
- Persist in the face of adversity
- Take tough decisions
- Don't duck when things go wrong

More to the point, charisma makes the job of leading easier. In today's fiercely competitive global economy, leaders need to energise their people more than ever. They have to encourage them to tackle the impossible and make them understand why change is constantly necessary, passionately explaining what's in it for them and the company. You can do this without charisma but the alternative takes a lot more of what companies don't have any more: time.

charisma makes the job of leading easier

Part 5

Putting it all together

This final part brings together the different aspects of the A-B-C approach to offer practical ways of applying new thinking and behaving in order to strengthen your Charisma Effect.

The four-step procedure offers a systematic approach in which you prepare, select, experiment and review to focus on change and alter your impact gradually.

Chapter 14

Using A-B-C in real life

The A-B-C of the Charisma Effect is a gentle, easy-to-use approach. Everything fits together, and so long as you recall the basic three elements you will start to make steady progress with an increased awareness of what produces a powerful and lasting impression.

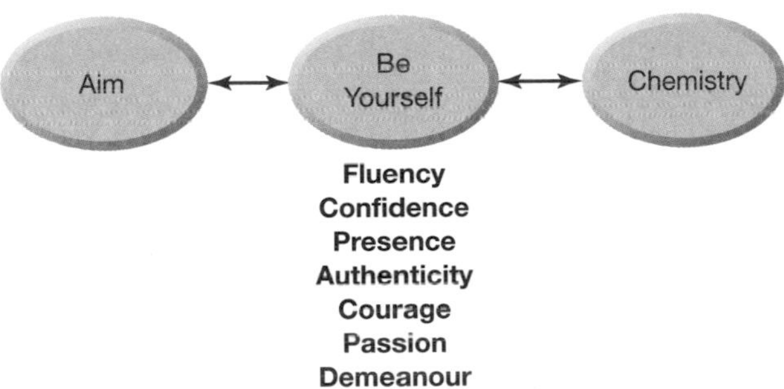

You cannot work on all of it at once, which is why exploring your profile (see Chapter 2) can be so useful in focusing on where to start.

There are two basic strategies you might consider adopting:

1 Focus on your known strengths and improve on them further.
2 Tackle specific development needs or weaknesses and work on these.

It is entirely your decision which approach you use, but usually some combination of both works best.

You can dip in and out of the various aspects of the A-B-C approach, using them as appropriate, but it could also be effective to use a four-step approach in applying it.

- **Step 1**: PREPARE to communicate with other people, including consciously holding the A-B-C framework firmly in your mind. Regularly remind yourself: Aim, Be yourself, Chemistry.
- **Step 2**: SELECT one of the key A-B-C behaviours or areas of development you want to work on – for example, confidence, passion, creating rapport, chemistry. Choose some practical actions to try out in the real-life situation.
- **Step 3**: EXPERIMENT with one or more of these new ways of interacting – for example using more open questions, more attentive listening, avoiding victim-type language or whatever.
- **Step 4**: REVIEW the results of your experiments. Consider further actions you might take.

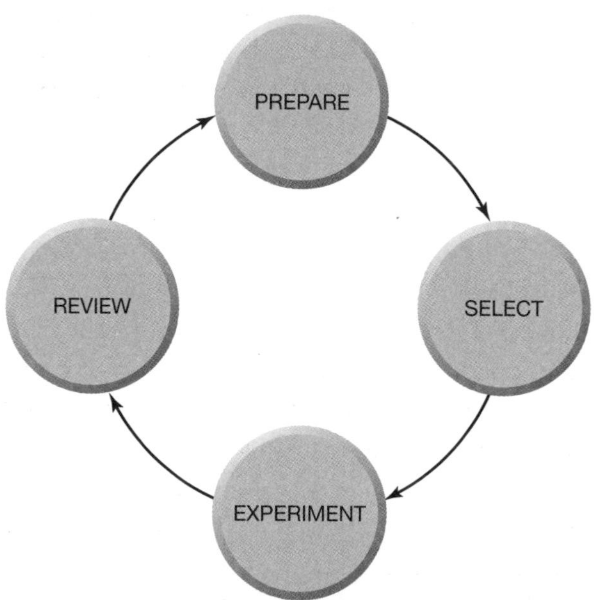

The A-B-C approach takes time to build into your regular interactions with other people, so avoid rushing it. Tackle the various issues you need to work at in very small bites, but keep at it, rather than leaving lots of gaps between your various experiments. In your daily interactions, keep checking on what is going on and what effect you seem to be having, how your audience seems to be thinking, feeling or behaving – reviewing the relationship dynamic.

tackle the various issues you need to work at in very small bites

At first, you may find it all a bit overwhelming as there is a lot to think about. As with all attempts at self-development it is usually best to avoid the 'big bang' approach of the New Year's resolution, setting an unrealistic target that is soon abandoned. Instead, go for small steps, constantly experiment and regularly review progress.

Eventually, the A-B-C approach becomes second nature – after all you are basically only reminding yourself: Aim – Be yourself – Chemistry, then focusing on one or perhaps two aspects of this at a time. This is what many of those with a strong impact do anyway, without thinking; it is so ingrained it happens automatically.

Have a plan

It can also help to create your own development plan, working systematically through the A-B-C framework. Here is an example.

- On Monday, pay special attention to your Aim in communication; explore what happens in various situations and how clear you are being and whether others seem to be clear about your messages and intentions.
- On Tuesday, pay special attention to one chosen aspect of the Be yourself set of behaviours. For example, you may decide to work on presence, and within that you might explore using the presence highway code from Chapter 5.

- On Wednesday, select a second aspect of your chosen Be yourself behaviour to work on. So, if yesterday you chose the highway code, perhaps today explore the use of your intuition; check on whether it serves you well or not.
- On Thursday and Friday, work on one or more elements of Chemistry: Attention, Interdependence or Rapport.
- At the weekend, tune in to all three elements of the A-B-C framework and review how it worked during the week. What have you learned from applying the framework and how did it affect your personal impact?

Alternatively you could adopt a rolling programme in which in the first week you focus on Aim, the second week on Be yourself, the third week on Chemistry and so on. Whatever plan you select, follow it over several weeks to experiment and see what you can achieve.

Below are some typical challenges where people want to make an impact, showing the approach in action.

Creating chemistry

Chemistry is the trickiest part of developing your charisma. Unlike Aim or Be yourself, you cannot 'do' chemistry: it is not a straightforward behaviour you can adopt. Instead, you need to invest in creating the two-way process of building a relationship with your audience.

chemistry is the trickiest part of developing your charisma

Now that you have a fuller understanding of what creates Chemistry, there are some practical actions you can take when using the A-B-C approach in any particular situation.

During your interactions with people, try recalling the essentials and use them as a mental checklist to assess what is happening *in the moment*, asking:

- 'Am I giving this relationship my energy – what might be stopping me doing that?'
- 'Am I promoting Rapport – is it happening and if not why not?'

Simply thinking about these while interacting with other people sharpens your awareness of what is happening. With increased awareness comes a better understanding of ways to positively affect the relationship dynamic.

Wrap up

If you have read this far, you now have access to the essential tools for transforming your charisma. In physical fitness training, you can seldom make a huge change in just a few visits to the gym. Instead, it usually works best by taking many small steps that eventually amount to a significant change. Much the same applies to developing your impact with other people. Small steps are usually best.

This is not a cookbook of best practice so much as a system for continuous personal growth. You will develop your impact by learning and experimenting as you go.

We live in an era that is perhaps most distinctive for its relentlessly accelerating pace of change. We are all part of that experience and if we are not individually to be left behind we must expect to keep changing too.

You already possess a natural ability to use your charisma; it just may not yet be at the level you want. So start experimenting with some of the ideas outlined in this book. Some will work and perhaps surprise you with how effective they are. Others may seem difficult, such as seeking feedback from colleagues, but ultimately all of them can be useful in the right circumstances.

Your charisma is not a fixed quantity – it has unlimited potential to grow and develop, depending on your commitment to positive action. Once a year a renowned golfer visits an old professional friend and, as if he were a beginner, says, 'Teach me to play golf.' Like that champion golfer, people who excel and make a strong and lasting impression are willing to keep looking for new ways to improve their impact still further.

your charisma is not a fixed quantity

Since there is no one right way to make a stunning personal impact, this gives you plenty of scope to use the A-B-C approach to explore this territory. Gradually you will uncover what works for you and what does not. As with any self-development it requires practice.

Improving your charisma should be high on your agenda, not for selfish reasons, but because it can help you achieve success in your career or whatever you attempt to do.

Of course, the A-B-C approach is not a magic solution, no panacea. It can steer you towards opportunities for making a stronger impression in an age where communicating well has become an essential skill for virtually everyone. As one person who kindly read an early draft of this book commented, 'I've simply become so much more aware of other people's behaviour and I've started to watch my own more carefully.'

Good luck!

> *'If you think you're too small to have an impact, try going to bed with a mosquito in the room.'*
>
> Anita Roddick, founder of the Body Shop

Notes

Introduction

1 *An Audience with Charisma*, Nikki Owen, www.audiencewith-charisma.com

Chapter 1

1 *Life*, Keith Richards, Weidenfeld & Nicolson (2010).
2 *The Dynamics of Persuasion: Communication and Attitudes in the 21st Century*, Richard M. Perloff, Lawrence Erlbaum Associates, Mahwah, NJ (2003).
3 *Guardian Weekend* column, Oliver Burkman, 21 July 2007.

Chapter 2

1 *Oscar Wilde*, Martin Fido, Hamlyn (1973).

Chapter 6

1 George, Bill, Sims, Peter, Mclean, Andrew N. and Meyer, Diana (2007); 'Discovering your authentic leadership', *Harvard Business Review*, Article R0702H, 1 February 2007.

Chapter 10

1 *Daily Mail* online, 12 October 2010.
2 'The Star Who Forgot to Shine', J. Queenan, *The Guardian*, 1 April 2011.
3 'Rupert Murdoch: 80-year-old Lenin launches a publishing revolution', *Money Week*, 16 February 2011.

Chapter 11

1 'Catching Charisma', Alana Conner, *Stanford Social Innovation Review*, Fall 2008.
2 'The smile that says where you're from', John Harlow, *Sunday Times*, 20 February 2005.

Chapter 13

1 'Why charismatic leaders are not always the answer', Dr Mike Rugg-Gunn, Human Asset Development, 2001.
2 'Does CEO Charisma Matter?', Bradley, R. Agle *et al.*, *Academy of Management Journal*, 2006, Vol. 49.
3 'The Unspoken Taboos of Leadership: Exploring Charisma', *Working Resources*, Vol. v, No. 7 newsletter.
4 'Why Should Anyone Be Led By You?, Robert Goffee and Gareth Jones, *Harvard Business Review*, September–October 2000.
5 'How to fake charisma', C. Kinsey Goman, Troy Media, 20 April 2011.
6 'Going out with a bang', *The Guardian*, 15 April 2011.

Index